MW01484183

A JOURNEY IN
BREATH

THE KNOWLEDGE, TECHNIQUES, AND EXERCISES TO MASTER YOUR BREATH AND BECOME A BADASS BREATHING WARRIOR

BRIAN M. WHITE

BAD TO BADASS (AN IMPRINT OF DARK REVELATIONS MEDIA LLC)

Copyright © 2023 by Brian M. White. All Right Reserved.

No part of this publication may be reproduced, distributed, or transmitted in any form or by any means, including photocopying, recording, or other electronic or mechanical methods, or by any information storage and retrieval system without the prior written permission of the publisher, except in the case of very brief quotations embodied in critical reviews and certain other noncommercial uses permitted by copyright law.

ISBN 978-1-944830-14-4

Published by Bad to Badass (An imprint of Dark Revelations Media LLC). For more information about authors and upcoming books visit: www.badtobadass.com

Disclaimer: The information presented herein is not specific medical advice for any individual and should not substitute medical advice from a health professional. If you have (or think you may have) a medical problem, speak to your doctor or health professional immediately about your risk and possible treatments. Do not engage in any exercise program, care or treatment without consulting a medical professional. Neither the author nor the publisher shall be liable or responsible for any loss or damages allegedly arising from any information or suggestions contained herein.

Contents

Introducing the Bad to Badass Series

M ost self-improvement, diet, wellness, or exercise books sell a system or program, locking you into a prescribed series of activities or actions designed to fix all your problems. Worse, these books often make it sound as if there is only **one** thing you must change in your life to make all your dreams come true. Whether it's diet, exercise, meditation, or finances, the authors of these books would have you believe that you just need to fix this one aspect of your life and everything else will take care of itself. Not so here. Change, and becoming the best version of yourself, takes time and effort. It is a campaign. There's no silver bullet. That is why this is just the first in a series of books equipping you with the tools you need on your journey to become your ultimate badass self. This book by itself will not fix you; that is up to you. It is simply meant to give you the knowledge, tools, and skills you will need to better yourself. It will outline a path, but you, the reader, must walk it.

With that said, I do believe that of all the books in this series, this one will give you the biggest bang for your buck. So long as you have the desire to improve your breathing, this book has the potential to dramatically better your health with very little time and effort. Is it a cure all? Nope. That is why this is only one in a series of books. I started it here because breathing properly was a challenge in my life and became a serious barrier to overcome if I was to reach my goal of obtaining optimal performance. Fixing my breathing drastically improved my health more than any other single change I've made to my life. My personal journey did not start here, but having learned what I have, I believe that proper breathing is what helped me truly turn the corner as I went from bad to badass.

How else is this series different? These books are first-hand accounts of how I went from bad to badass. I'm not going to bore you with a lot of physiology, biology, chemistry, and math. I view self-improvement as both art and science, and as such I did a lot of hands-on research, using what worked and throwing out the rest. These books include what worked for me, distilled down to its bare essence, along with the techniques, tips, and tricks I used to become efficient and effective. I wanted to create a framework and provide the building blocks, so you can then tweak the techniques and advice to best meet your individual needs and goals.

Second, I don't spend a lot of time telling you why things may work from a biological perspective. I will present the fundamental knowledge necessary to give you an understanding of proper breathing and how particular breathing patterns and exercises can change your biology and physiology. For those that are interested in diving deeper, I will point you to additional resources to learn more.

Personally, I use some very simple methods for gauging progress. Some are objective, like a BOLT score (more on this later) or number of sets and repetitions; but, more often, I gauge progress by how I feel. Subjective, I know, but part of getting better isn't about just improving the numbers; it's also about improving how you feel and how you perform. There are plenty of books that explain the science behind the why and how things work. The reason I focus on breath-work exercises and techniques is because I want to lower the barrier of entry for change. I want people to understand that by making some simple changes they can begin to dramatically improve their health and optimize their lives. I want people to realize that they are in control of their lives and health. Once that initial investment pays off, I have found that people are willing to invest more time and effort into becoming badass. And that is the ultimate goal of this series.

Many people who know me feel I live a very Spartan, uncomfortable existence because of my routines, and the challenges I constantly impose on myself. Get comfortable with being uncomfortable is rule one. If change was easy, everyone would be doing it. However, it's never as hard as other people make it out to be. My response to people believing I live life the "hard way" is, "If you could feel the way I feel, you would do the things I do." Whether it's taking cold baths, long training sessions, barefoot running, breathwork, meditation, diet, etc., it's worth it because of how these things make me feel. How do they make me feel? Ready, willing, and able to take on the next obstacle in my path. In short – badass!

Usually when I talk to people about self-improvement they tell me that they start out strong and then tire quickly because they don't get the payoff. When I look at what programs they use, I have found that they either start too small or too big. To feel a difference, in whatever you do, you have to reach critical mass, which is that turning point where you have put in enough time and effort to start seeing and feeling the results. Getting there is a balancing act. Too little won't get you there, and too much will crush you before you do. Part of the problem is motivation. You can't immediately feel the benefits without doing the work. Unfortunately, I can't make you feel the way I feel. If you don't trust me, you may not be willing to put in the effort to realize the payout is real. I promise you it is, but I'm going to have a hard time convincing you of that just by saying it. I can't distill that badass feeling into a pill to make you feel what I feel and prove this journey is worth it. I'm also not going to ask you to take my word for it. Instead, I'm asking you to make a small investment. Which is why this series begins here; to gain your trust, I'm starting off with what I believe gives you the biggest bang for your buck. Very little effort and time will lead to a large payout. From there, we will learn to trust each other and can start working together on the path of becoming badass.

Be open minded. Be willing to change. Put in the work. Those are the only requirements.

Let's begin.

MY JOURNEY IN BREATH

It was October, brisk but not as seasonally cold as usual for northern New Jersey. There was a dampness to the air that once would have caused my lungs to seize as I reached for my asthma inhaler. But not today. Today was a day for epiphanies and victories. It was neither the beginning nor end of a long journey but a significant milestone on the path. It was a moment of awe, when I knew the miraculous had happened and I was on the verge of completing something most people, including myself, said I'd never be capable of doing.

As I started jogging down the muddy hill toward the line of fire that was the final obstacle on my way to finishing my second Spartan Obstacle Course race within 30 hours, I had a type of awakening. I had, crawled, climbed, carried buckets filled with stone and bags of sand, and overcome 55 obstacles while running more than 20 miles of rough, mountainous terrain. This line of fire was the last hurdle. As if that wasn't enough, I would later learn that out of the 4,000 participants that raced that weekend (about 2,000 in the Spartan Beast, a 21K 30+ obstacle race, and 2,000 in the Spartan Super, a 10K 25+ obstacle race) I'd finished in the top 10% in the open categories in both races overall. To me this was a great accomplishment. (Sidenote: At 190 pounds I'm no gazelle and not a great runner, but I love the atmosphere and "badassedness" of Spartan events and the people that compete in them. I highly recommend trying one.) Seven years prior, when I started this journey, I competed in a 5K Spartan Sprint that took me more than three hours. Today my time on the 10K Super was 2:22:53 and on the 21K Beast the previous day I clocked in at 4:25:33.

That transformation and the journey I had taken to get there was what I thought about as I raced down the slope in the hills of Vernon, New Jersey. Although I only began to fully unravel and appreciate what I had accomplished in the coming days, it was that moment where I realized something important had occurred. And what was it that made this moment so important to me, filling me with the feeling of overwhelming gratitude? I could breathe, and for someone who was diagnosed with chronic asthma at the age of 10, that was a gift I did not take for granted.

As I jumped over the flames and claimed my second finisher medal of the weekend, I had never felt more grateful. Any asthmatic will tell you they never take breathing for granted. I didn't, and I wouldn't. Having just accomplished a goal, that had exceeded the expectations of all the naysayers, I decided that I also wanted to make sure others no longer took breathing for granted either.

How did this journey get started?

I'm not a naturally gifted athlete or superman. I'm like many others. I have a family, full-time job, and hobbies. I've always enjoyed various physical activities, such as powerlifting and mountain biking, but it was only much later that I realized I'd never lived up to my potential when it came to fitness and athletics. This realization led me on this journey, which started for me, maybe later than it does for others, in my forties. Everyone starts from somewhere with certain baggage or challenges; but we can all improve, we can all strive to become the best versions of ourselves, and that's what I was committed to doing. So what prompted such a revelation that made me determined to make myself better? As with most people, it was when I was confronted by a painful truth. I had to either change or accept defeat – and I refused to be defeated.

Asthma drugs have come a long way since I was a child. When I was a kid most preventative inhalers were hard to use and didn't seem all that effective. Rescue inhalers like albuterol had not changed much in the 30 years since my diagnosis. My bathroom was always stocked with a nebulizer, inhalers, and anti-inflammatory steroids like prednisone. Finally, when I was in my early thirties, the pharmaceuticals got better and I began to experience what life could be like without having to go through the terror of an attack, which happened whenever I tried to do something physical. Soccer, running, mountain biking, wrestling always came with an attack. It was just a matter of how bad it would get and how many hits of an albuterol inhaler I would have to take to make it go away. Steroid preventative inhalers mitigated this for a time, and for a moment I saw the sun. I knew what it felt like to breathe without fear. Unfortunately, that time in the sun did not last long.

But I'll get to that. First off, I'm an outdoor person, always have been – hiking, BMX, soccer – but my asthma was troublesome. I've been to emergency rooms, hospitalized at times, just because I'd left my inhaler in another pair of jeans and by the time I got to it, the attack was so bad I couldn't even breathe enough medicine into my lungs for it to be effective. To my parents' credit they encouraged all my activities. As a parent myself I realize how difficult it must have been for them to watch their child play soccer, holding an inhaler in their hands, wondering if he was going to have an attack; or, worse, have to be rushed to the hospital. It would have been easier for them if I'd been a video-game junkie, but they encouraged me nonetheless. Yet another thing I'm grateful for.

But it wasn't easy, and there were times when I wondered if I was spitting into the wind. Maybe I just needed to accept my disease and take it easy. Luckily, that wasn't in me either. However, in the short term I definitely had some setbacks. In high school I tried football, lasted half a season and then needed knee surgery. I wrestled and would always have to take a medical time out to take a puff of my inhaler hoping it would take effect before I had to get back on the mat. But I never had control of my breathing. I was always gasping. I had little to no cardio capacity, and if I ever made it the full six minutes of a match, which felt like an eternity in hell, I would be dizzy and gasping with my heart racing at more than 180 beats per minute from the multiple inhaler hits. My hands would be shaking and I'd feel overwhelming anxiety. This feeling would haunt me well past the end of the match.

At some point I began to let fear get the best of me. The terror that came from not being able to catch my breath and running out of air overwhelmed me. I stopped. I gave in. If that wasn't bad enough, I then started some bad habits as if attempting to sabotage my health. I started smoking cigarettes, like any idiot with asthma would. I gave up on any type of aerobic activity and focused on powerlifting. Even a heavy set of bench would have me winded. It was not one of the shining periods of my life.

Eventually, I'd get my head on straight and quit smoking. Wanting to get back into a healthier lifestyle, I went to the doctor who prescribed some new asthma treatments and, for a time, it felt like being reborn. The preventative inhalers allowed me to engage in activities without waiting for the other shoe to drop. I needed my rescue inhaler less and less. Downhill mountain biking became my new passion. Although the medication prevented attacks I still had no cardio or lung capacity. Downhill was great because I didn't have to do long climbs which resulted in me gasping for air. No matter how much I trained, my cardio never improved, but I had few attacks and wasn't wheezing (which made it feel like I was trying to breathe through the multiple filters of a gas mask).

I loved downhill mountain biking and then also got into snow-boarding and rock climbing. I felt I should stick with these because they did not require a ton of heavy cardio. I blamed my lack of cardio fitness on asthma, but in truth it was caused by ignorance (as I would find out much later). Asthma starts a vicious cycle, and it's hard to determine which is the chicken and which the egg. Struggling to breathe during an attack results in bad breathing habits, which cause worse asthma symptoms, which lead to even worse breathing habits, and the cycle continues. Each revolution of this cycle results in a worsening of both conditions. I would learn this later, but at the time I was just grateful that I could breathe well enough to enjoy the outdoors without having severe attacks, having my sleep disrupted by wheezing, or waking up dripping with sweat as I struggled to catch my breath while searching the nightstand for my rescue inhaler.

Slowly but surely the benefits of the medications waned. I started having attacks again; first sporadically, then more frequently, then the albuterol Inhaler wasn't helping as much or I had to take more of it. There were higher doses, more frequent uses, and more helpings of prednisone as the incidence of upper respiratory infections increased. Every time I got the sniffles it would move to the weakest area of my body, the lungs, and it would be a cycle of antibiotics and prednisone, both of which also came with side effects that were affecting my health. With all this, my ability to engage in the activities I loved was being hampered. In the end, the advice from doctors was to start to take life a little slower, "Your lungs were just not built for those activities."

Unfortunately, my mind and spirit were and I could not contemplate life without the mountains, hiking, or biking.

I entered a dark night of the soul. I was contemplating not just giving up activities I loved but also what my life would be like as I got older. I had just entered my forties, and I was forced to contemplate slowing down and taking it easy. Even then, there would be more and more medications to take, all of which had serious side effects on my lungs, gut health, and heart. If I couldn't do the things I loved now, where was I going to be in 10 or 20 years' time? My mortality and the life-changing nature of breathing suddenly came to the front and center of my consciousness. Asthma was beating me, and unless there was a cure, it was going to affect the rest of my life, however short that life was beginning to look. In many ways I felt helpless, defeated.

I learned over the course of the next few years that there is a cure, one that had nothing to do with doctors, medications, or genetic research and manipulation. Asthma would affect the course of my life but not in the way I had assumed. Asthma would change my life for the better, forcing me to analyze my health, learn about my condition, and, ultimately, take control of my health and learn how to breathe. I've never taken the ability to draw air into my lungs for granted, and on this journey I would learn to become grateful for every blessed breath.

THE HOW OF BREATHING AND BECOMING BADASS

There are a lot of books about breathing. Many of those I have read explore the science and techniques of breathing in more depth from a physiological perspective. I heartily recommend checking out the, *Where to Learn More about Breathing* section at the end of this book, if you are the type of person that needs to know the why of something. This will point you to a suggested reading list on breathing biology, chemistry, and physiology if that is your thing. This book, however, focuses on the how. How can I become a badass breather? I will cover the techniques I use and how they help my breathing performance. I will show which techniques I use on a daily and weekly basis to not only rid me of my asthma but make it possible for me to accomplish things that friends, family, doctors and even I did not think were possible before I embarked on this journey.

In each section I'll cover my experience with the techniques, training, and how it helped me. In some ways the chapters are out of order. If I knew everything that I know now then I would have started with some of the techniques I learned later down the road, because of their wide sweeping impacts to my health. However, I chose to write this book in the order in which I learned and experienced it.

What I can say with confidence is that you will not likely find a stronger advocate for the importance of breathing. This is not just a book for asthmatics, although I hope these lessons and my journey will aid any asthmatics in experiencing the freedom I now have. Ultimately, this is a book for all those who want to live better and not take a single breath for granted.

On my journey to completing more than 25 Spartan races and mountain biking (I can do long trail rides now) on a weekly basis, there have been many changes in my life. I am not claiming that breathing is the only thing (that ever elusive silver bullet), but it was the first thing and the core thing that enabled everything that followed. Even after making changes in diet and exercise I always struggled with my breathing and cardio, and it wasn't until I learned to breathe properly and train my breathing that I unlocked my body's full potential. As an example, when I completed those two back-to-back Spartan races I had been dieting and exercising regularly for more than six years. The only thing I added to my preparation for that challenge was breathing exercises. All my other preparations were the same but for that one thing. And it made all the difference.

As much as this book includes information about breathing and techniques to improve it, it is also meant as an inspirational story of how focusing on breath can change your life and may be the key to unlocking hidden potential you didn't even know you possessed. That is why I wrote this book. To give thanks to breathing, and to those that have devoted a lot of their time and effort in sharing their techniques for breathing and its importance in performance. I wanted to write this to ensure I would never take breath for granted, and I hope after reading this you won't either.

BREATHING ASSESSMENT AND REACHING CRITICAL MASS: WHERE ARE YOU NOW – BAD, BASE, OR BADASS?

There are many ways to assess your current status in regards to breathing. One is the body oxygen level test (BOLT) score. This is a simple test created and popularized by Patrick McKeown in his book, *The Oxygen Advantage*. It is a relative indicator of breathing volume during rest. Low BOLT scores means high breathing volume, which would indicate more breathlessness during exercise. This may sound contradictory at the moment, but we'll get into how breathing volume affects breathing performance and oxygen absorption later. For now, it may be beneficial to know what your score is. This test is performed while at rest with a resting heart rate (not right after exercise). For consistency I always perform this after waking and before I get out of bed.

Slowly breathe in through your nose and then exhale normally. At the completion of the exhale, lightly pinch your nose and start timing for how long you can hold your breath before you feel the urge to breathe. For this assessment, an urge to breathe could be characterized by an urge to swallow, involuntary contraction of your diaphragm or abdominal muscles, or a strong involuntary urge to take a breath. This is not a test of how long you can hold your breath, but how long your body can go before experiencing the need to breathe. So put your ego aside because the only person you will be fooling will be yourself.

Now, normal BOLT scores are in the area of 20-40 seconds. Most athletes without breathwork training get around 20 seconds, but that is suboptimal. The goal should be 30-40 seconds for a badass. What was mine when I first started? I didn't find out about the BOLT scoring till about halfway through this journey, and when I did it was eight! Yes, that's eight seconds! By using the exercises in this book, my BOLT score is now 32. It took a little over a year to get there. However, with each five-second rise in BOLT score I noticed a significant difference in my performance, and I believe you will too.

That is the only truly objective measure I use for performance. However, I also urge you to ask yourself the following questions as further points of assessment:

- Do I breathe through my mouth?

- Do I snore when I sleep?

- Do I breathe through my chest and pull in my abdomen, raising my shoulders, when I breathe hard (such as during or after intense exercise)?

- Is my breath the first thing to give out when I exercise?

- Does it seem that my cardio never improves even though I run, bike, swim, etc. regularly?

- Is my BOLT score below 20?

If the answer is yes to any of these questions, then this book can help. Because if you are not breathing properly you are not performing optimally and you are pushing a boulder up a hill when you could be sprinting down it. That is no way to become badass.

I personally could answer yes to all the above questions and throughout this journey have constantly assessed myself. However, that inventory was more subjective. Life, to me, is art, and I didn't want to reduce it to a number. Some people like to gauge performance objectively. I do this with weight lifting, but for all other things I tend to look at where I was and where I am now, with an eye towards where I'd like to be in the future. Therefore, it's subjective to a certain degree. I keep journals that show how long some of my breath holds were, my BOLT score, and number of repetitions I could perform in certain exercises while holding my breath; but, at the end of the day, what really matters is how I'm performing today and whether I'm doing what I can to ensure that I will be performing better tomorrow. To me, that is badass.

With that said, I believe most people don't make progress because they fail to put in the time and effort required to begin reaping the rewards. Why? Because they start something but quit before they reach critical mass. Critical mass? Yes, that concept I brought up a few pages ago. Critical mass is the point where the work you put in starts to pay dividends, and instead of grudgingly sacrificing time to engage in these activities and healthy habits, you are making time because you have experienced the benefits. The damage caused by years of bad breathing will not be repaired in a day. But I'm not asking for much in terms of time, pain, and money. Yet the rewards from breathing properly are huge. It's a no-brainer. However, I would say that you should first read this book all the way through and then start some of the breathing corrections and exercises immediately. Within two to four weeks you should see your BOLT score rising, and once it increases by five points I believe you will notice a difference. So please don't give up; read about my journey and how it has improved my life, and commit the time and effort (which I promise is minimal) to reach critical mass (increasing your BOLT score by a minimum of five points). Once you reach critical mass the dividends will keep paying off and you'll want to increase your investments. This is the start.

Chapter 1 - A Cold Teacher

It's 5:30 am, dark, and really cold at 25 degrees Fahrenheit, especially when you consider that I am clad in only a pair of shorts. There is a slight breeze which feels like knives cutting across my skin as I sit cross-legged on my front stoop and look at the timer running on my smartphone. By the way, I hate the cold, and I'm only 10 minutes into a 30-minute ordeal. This is the beginning of my journey from bad to badass. Cold therapy. If you told me that a year from that moment I would be taking a cold shower every morning, or would look forward to submerging myself in the frozen tub of ice sitting on my deck, I would have wheezed out some sarcastic reply. Basically, I would have said, "No way, that's insane, not going to happen."

If there is one thing I have learned throughout this journey it is that we as humans are capable of much more than we think we are. With every step on this journey, I broke through barriers both mental and physical that had seemed insurmountable just moments before.

So why was I sitting out in the cold in a pair of shorts? Why indeed! At that moment it did not seem like a wise plan or a path to better breathing.

About a month prior I had been forced to turn around only three miles into what would usually be a 10 to 14-mile mountain bike trail ride. Why? The cold, and how my lungs reacted to it. Cold air had a way of immediately sparking off my asthma. On that first breath of cold air my lungs would cramp up, and then the wheezing would start. I'd have to take at least one albuterol inhaler hit before even starting the ride, and it didn't always get better from there; sometimes, it got a lot worse. This was one of those days where it kept getting worse, and it felt like I was risking a heart attack to take any more medication in order to continue the ride. Truth was the inhaler didn't seem to be doing anything anyway, other than make my heart race.

I'd already taken three double shots and was still laboring. I could feel my heart hammering in my chest. When I paid attention to it I felt dizzy, scared. I was having a panic attack. I was out in the middle of the forest, about to have a heart attack and die in the cold, alone. I slowly walked back to the car, defeated and afraid. Wondering with each step if it would be my last.

Every time I get home my wife asks if I've had a good ride. My ritual answer had always been, "The only bad ride is the one you don't go on." And I believed it. Mangled bike, broken kneecap, dislocated shoulder, those were just the consequences of flow and mountain biking. If you don't ride you can't get hurt, but you also don't get the fulfillment that comes with it. That is why every ride, even those that ended in pain, were far better than the ride not taken. I wouldn't have it any other way. But not that day. That day had not been fun, and for the first time I began to wonder if my mountain biking days were coming to an end.

I needed to do something. I was on a preventative inhaler, used a rescue inhaler a minimum of five times a day, took prednisone at least twice a year whenever I got a cold to fend off a respiratory infection, and I still couldn't breathe right. I still couldn't perform the way I wanted. My muscles and body were strong but my heart and lungs could no longer drive them. I'd researched new therapies, switched medications and yet here I was, still out of breath. Defeated. None of it was working.

With that in mind I decided to trawl the Internet, but I wasn't searching for new asthma treatments or medications. I was looking for breathing exercises, and the name at the top of the list was Wim Hof. The King of Cold, whose infamous catch phrase, "Just breathe, motherfucker," had sparked a revolution of sorts. If there is anything that can be said about Wim, it's that his enthusiasm and passion for living life to the fullest is contagious, and for him it all started with breathing and cold. Hence my December morning bathing party.

The Wim Hof method is very similar to Tummo breathing in yoga where you are taking in quick, deep breaths (hyperventilating) then letting go of the breath without forcing a contraction of the breathing muscles on the exhale. You perform this rapid breathing for 30-40 cycles and then take a large breath in, filling your whole body. You then push all the air out of your lungs and hold that empty-lung breath for as long as possible. Once it becomes uncomfortable, you take in a deep breath and then hold that breath (full lungs) for 15-30 seconds. That is one complete cycle. You then start from the beginning, taking 30-40 quick, hyperventilating breaths, breathe deep, breathe completely out, hold, breathe in, hold for 15-30 seconds, release, and repeat for three or four complete cycles. This became known to me as the Wim Hof method, which was the foundation for all of my breathwork that would follow. In the advance techniques section at the end of this chapter, I'll detail how I've incorporated additional techniques and breathing patterns to this core method; but this was, and continues to be, one of my core breathing practices. I do this every single morning without fail. If it is the only breathing exercise I do in a day, I consider that I have met the standard.

On that cold December morning, as I hyperventilated and then held my breath with empty lungs, I made it 35 seconds before having to breathe. I tried not to focus on the time or the cold. I could feel my fingers and toes begin to get tingly after the first cycle. During the breath hold on the second cycle I did not feel the immediate need to take a breath and, strangely enough, when I checked in with my body I didn't feel cold either. Then a swallow, the urge to breathe. I flatten my stomach, contract my abdominals, keeping that intake of breath at bay. I open my eyes: one minute, 10 seconds. I take in a huge breath, hold for 30 seconds, and then begin hyperventilating again.

This is the third and final cycle. I begin to actually feel warm; the cold breeze no longer slices my skin like a set of sharpened knives but becomes a bellow that further stokes the fires within. I begin to picture in my mind's eye that the wind creates heat when it hits my body. That visualization becomes more and more concrete as I continue to breathe. As I breathe out and hold, I close my eyes. In the darkness I am calm, my body feels alive. My internal voice is quiet, the engines of alchemy and transmutation turn air into heat, into life, without me needing to force it. It is another type of intelligence, a body awareness grounded in its assurance that it knows what to do and when.

There is the gentle reminder to breathe, and I open my eyes: one minute 45 seconds. I breathe in. Hold. Breathe out. My first Wim Hof breathing session complete and no inhaler needed.

Why does this method allow you to hold your breath for longer durations than you thought were possible? Hyperventilation causes the release of more carbon dioxide through quick respiration, creating an alkaline blood pH. As we hold our breath, carbon dioxide levels rise until we feel the need to breathe again. Because the blood pH was made more alkaline during the hyperventilation phase of the Wim Hof method, it takes longer for those levels to begin to rise again during the hold; but they never reach baseline levels, which decreases the body's hunger for air and need to breathe. During each successive cycle, the carbon dioxide levels stay lower, which allows for longer breath holds while keeping the blood more alkaline.

Secondly, a substance called nitric oxide, which we will see again when we talk about the nose, is also released during the breath holds. This acts as a vasodilator which enlarges our capillaries, allowing for greater oxygen absorption. The more oxygen absorption per breath, the more oxygen delivered to your muscles to perform work. In addition, the higher your oxygen absorption rate, the fewer breaths you need to sustain a particular workload. This further reduces stress on your cardiorespiratory system.

During this exercise you will experience the effects of this oxygenation and decrease in carbon dioxide as a tingling sensation in hands, feet, and lips. I also pair this exercise with meditation because it can also bring about a feeling of calm and euphoria.

Was my asthma cured? No. Could I bike without an inhaler? No. Did my breathing improve? Absolutely. Within a month of doing three cycles every morning in the cold, I cut down my rescue inhaler usage by half, and could safely do a 10- to 14-mile mountain bike ride without fearing a heart attack from inhaler overuse, which subsequently benefited me by reducing my anxiety and panic attacks. The most important benefit, however, was that I began to realize that I was on to something. I'd been looking for the wrong type of treatments. The fact that the body had innate abilities to heal itself had only occurred to me on a theoretical level; I'd never believed it could actually work. I had been told that I had a disease that was most likely genetic. I was broken. My body was not designed to function properly. And with the Wim Hof method, all those assumptions had been challenged. I was on a new path.

I had discovered that regulating my breathing and performing this simple technique for just 15-20 minutes every morning could boost my immune system, reduce inflammation, and allow me to start relying less on my medications and more on my body's natural abilities. This was an eye opener. In addition, I realized that it also affected my mood. The exercise enlivened me, woke me up, almost more so than my morning coffee, and at the same time was capable of shutting the mouth of the constantly chattering, negative, critical idiot that hid in my brain. All this by changing how I breathed. This was the revelation that sparked a journey, because now I wanted to find out what else I was missing.

If you look into the science of the Wim Hof method, you will find that doing the cycles changes your blood pH while also increasing the time it takes for carbon dioxide levels to rise back to normal. All of this helps to balance the body's need for oxygen while also aiding in the reduction of inflammation. This breathing pattern combined with the cold, the stress of which prompts your body to marshal a natural immune response, is a powerful tool that will go a long way to staving off autoimmune diseases such as asthma. In my case, my asthma was often triggered by environmental conditions like cold or sudden stress. By constantly exposing myself to these conditions in a manner that allowed my immune system to adapt, I began to reduce my need for medications, which had a synergistic effect because it also changed how I breathed.

As I am writing this now, that first Wim Hof breathing session was eight years ago. It was the beginning of my journey, and even today I continue to practice the Wim Hof method every morning. I have added some nuances which I will detail in the advanced techniques section. Today, I can do a four-minute empty breath hold, and you will frequently find me sitting in a 150-gallon tub of natural ice in the winter every morning for five to 15 minutes.

Knee problems, shoulder pain, sciatica, back stiffness, which had started to become debilitating at times, disappeared within weeks of doing daily cold-water submersion. I will speak more about the cold as an anti-inflammatory, an important part of muscle recovery, and immune system stimulator in a future badass book; but this book is about breathing, and the cold can teach you how to breathe.

I still had problems. My asthma was still there. Led by Wim, however, I now had a path to follow and officially started my journey towards finding natural solutions to heal my breathing.

Key Takeaways

- How we breathe effects how we function as human beings. It affects our health, our performance, our emotions.

- Taking control of how we breathe allows us to control things we previously thought were out of our control, which is a revelation in and of itself.

- Be aware of how you breathe. Be conscious of it. Pay attention to how you breathe in certain situations, when you are angry, depressed, anxious. As we become aware and proceed on this journey, we will discover methods for controlling these states or mitigating them with breath. But awareness must come first.

- Because of its ability to reduce carbon dioxide levels and create a more alkaline blood pH, the Wim Hof method does not increase tolerance to rising carbon dioxide levels, which we will learn later can be one cause of our need to overbreathe to relieve a feeling of consistent air hunger. To combat this effect, other breath-holding techniques should be added to your daily routine, which we will cover in later chapters.

Core Techniques

Sit or lie down in a safe place where if you get dizzy you are not in danger of falling or hitting something. Feeling tingling in your fingers, toes, and lips is normal, as is the potential for light-headedness. So be safe. I've seen lessons where there is no regard for whether or not you breathe out of nose or mouth, and some that even prefer mouth breathing. As I'll explain later, I do most exercises breathing through the nose with only a few exceptions. This is not one of those exceptions, so I suggest doing this exercise exclusively using nose breathing.

Take a deep, quick, belly breath in through the nose, using your diaphragm to fill your lungs from bottom to top. During these breaths you can place a hand on your stomach to ensure that you are breathing primarily through your diaphragm. Stretch your midsection out, filling it up as much as possible during the inhale.

On the exhale, relax. Do not push the breath out. Just let the air out naturally through your nose. This should not be a full exhale. Simply relax and let the breath out before quickly breathing in again. This exercise is basically controlled hyperventilation so inhales and exhales are rapid and sharp.

Breathe in again. Try to increase the pace and depth slightly with each breath. Feel your belly expanding further, the air filling your lungs; with each breath the air rises, moving all the way to your neck and head, oxygen filling your whole body. **Breathe like this for 30-40 repetitions.**

Take in a deep breath, filling your belly, lungs, body; pull the breath all the way to the top of your head. Pause. And then release. On this exhalation, relax but fully exhale, emptying your lungs. At the bottom of the breath when there is no air left, hold. Hold this breath for as long as possible. A minute or so is average when first starting. Once the urge to breathe becomes overwhelming, or at least uncomfortable, take in a deep nose/belly breath and, with full lungs, hold for 15-30 seconds. Let the breath out.

That completes round one.

Without any rest, begin your 30-40 deep belly breaths to begin round two.

Rinse, wash, and repeat for three or four rounds. With each round you should be able to hold your empty-lung breath for longer. Typically, mine increases by 30-60 seconds on each cycle.

I have found that this is best done in the morning before eating. This is my favorite exercise and wakes me up more than my coffee. I'm ready to take on the day, oxygenated, awake, and in a great frame of mind. Not a bad way to kick things off.

Advanced Techniques

As I stated previously, the Wim Hof method is at the core of my breathwork. With that in mind I began to make my own additions to the technique. Throughout this book I will show ways in which to combine techniques to create synergistic compound exercises. I will also offer suggestions and ideas for incorporating these techniques into your daily life and workout routines. You then can't use the excuse of saying you don't have the time for breathwork. In the 20-30 minutes I spend every morning doing the Wim Hof method, I'm able to meditate, visualize, massage my organs, give my abs a workout, and do pelvic floor exercises. Some of these advanced techniques will incorporate exercises or patterns that will be covered in more detail later in the book, so for now you can just use them as reference and come back to them later after you are comfortable with the core technique. This will be true for all the exercises in this book. Build a solid base and get comfortable with the core technique before moving on to the advanced techniques, adding variations, or performing your own tweaks.

Advanced Technique Variation 1

During the empty-lung breath hold, every time you feel an urge to breathe, let out a small flicker of air through your nose. While doing so hollow out your middle, pulling in your abs while tightening them, like in a crunch. This will prevent taking in an involuntary breath as you push out; continue doing this as the air hunger builds. As you hollow out, begin to push the contractions further down into your pelvic floor (your bicycle seat muscles). Picture the connection between your diaphragm, abdominal muscles, and pelvic muscles. As you continue push down on these muscles, contracting them as you exhale. Think of this as a reverse Kegel exercise. Instead of pulling in and up as you would with a Kegel exercise, you are pushing down on those areas of your pelvic floor, those same muscles that would rest on a bicycle seat. Continue with these contractions until you can no longer hold your breath.

As you breathe in, fill your diaphragm while releasing and relaxing your pelvic floor. I do not do this for all three cycles but usually choose one cycle. I may also combine this with some of the other variations that follow. This allows you to work your exhale muscles, your abdominals, and your pelvic floor all in one cycle.

Advanced Technique Variation 2

For the first three to five hyperventilation breaths I will force all the air out of my lungs, hollow out, and pull my abdominal muscles up and in. Very gently I will use my fingers to massage the organs below the ribs down to the belly button almost in a tickling motion, pushing in only slightly as I continue to hollow out. This massage helps digestion as well as other processes that will be covered in more depth in Chapter 3.

Advanced Technique Variation 3

For the first 20 breaths I fill my diaphragm first and, once I've taken a full belly breath, I will move the air up into my chest, attempting to get it all the way up to just below my collarbone. The upper chest should move slightly as you do this. When I relax to exhale, I release the upper chest first, the air moving down as the diaphragm then releases. Do not contract or use a forceful exhale; this is simply a letting go, only with control on the pattern of relaxation with upper chest first, then the belly. This may take some practice. Visualize the movement of pulling air up from the belly to the upper chest and throat. With enough practice I have found that the breathing muscles automatically figure out how to perform this pattern.

After 20 breaths I then do the standard 20 additional breaths using diaphragmatic breathing, with emphasis on expanding my midsection more with each breath so that I'm breathing around my entire middle. On the last breath in, I again pull the air all the way up to my throat, to the tip of my head, hold for a moment and then release into the empty-lung breath hold.

This variation will introduce you to controlling the movement of air to different parts of your lungs and to fill them completely from bottom to top. This will become a key skill to develop as you move on to more difficult breathing patterns later in the book.

Advanced Technique Variation 4

Not so much a variation as some suggestions for adding some meditation into your breathwork session. You will find an amazing silence in this practice during the empty-lung breath hold. All life makes noise: breathing, your heart beating. But when you quieten that noise, where even the sound of respiration disappears, there is calmness. This can put you in a perfect place to either let go and allow that silence to calm you or use visualization techniques, mantras, or whatever you like to fill that space. At times I have been able to hear my heart and pay attention to the pulse. At other times I visualize healing parts of my body that ache, or a perfect lift, race, day at work, whatever the case. This time is not wasteful, but some of the calmest moments of my day. It is a silence that can be very healing, pulling you into the importance of the moment.

Chapter 2 - Breathe in the Box

B reathe in a box? Not literally. But I'll get to that.

My journey up till this point was guided by the popularity of techniques and their ability to make it to page one of a Google search. Box breathing is mentioned in almost all of the breathing books I have read, as well as in quite a few meditation, sports training, self-improvement, and stress management books I came across.

Why so popular? It's simple, and it works.

As I had discovered with the Wim Hof method, breathing could affect me, both physically and mentally. I experienced most of the benefits physically: tolerance to cold, more efficient immune system, and an increase in energy and focus. It could also bring on periods of calm which I attributed to the absolute silence of the body when performing extended breath holds.

With box breathing I began to experience a deeper understanding of how breath could affect both my mental and emotional responses. This appealed to me because I'm highly-strung, tend towards pessimism and anger, and have a history of anxiety and panic attacks. What is the usual prescription for these symptoms (assuming we are removing pharmaceutical interventions)? You guessed it, meditation! "Really? Meditation. Wow, I wish I'd thought of that." This was my typical sarcastic response after having received that advice for the thousandth time. I'd then follow it up with a I-should've-had-a-V8 slap to the forehead for good measure. I thought I was going to punch the next person that said, "Why don't you try meditation?" Now that's anger management for you. To be fair these people were genuinely concerned and trying to help, but when you are a long-term sufferer of a condition and someone mentions the same thing that every other person has, a level of frustration and hopelessness begins to settle in.

Truth was this reaction was born more from my frustration with myself. Each time I explained what I was going through I'd hoped the person would have a new idea, because I'd tried meditation and it hadn't worked or I wasn't doing it right. Either way it was rare that anyone gave me different advice. The prescription usually went something like this: change your diet, avoid caffeine, exercise more, meditate, do yoga, and my personal favorite, "Just relax." I had tried all these and none had worked, which only increased the belief that something was really wrong with me. To add insult to injury, medications like albuterol inhalers, prednisone, and the inhaled anti-inflammatory steroids found in many preventative inhalers, tend to increase anxiety. Put 10 to 20 puffs of albuterol on top of a few cups of coffee and if you didn't have a heart attack you certainly would end up a little jumpy, walking around with a short fuse that was just waiting to be lit.

As you can see, my problems, as with most people, have a way of compounding. Bad breathing led to asthma, which led to medications, which led to anxiety, which led to even worse breathing, a vicious downward spiral towards the drain. It was a synergistic shit machine with each "remedy" causing an imbalance that threw something else further out of balance. In this case, my asthma meant I didn't breathe properly, necessitating the need for medication that caused stress in a person with a tendency towards pessimism, anxiety, and anger.

To me meditation was a sit in the lotus position and clear your mind type of thing. But my mind was never clear, except ... Except when performing breath holds using the Wim Hof method. This realization is what prompted me to search for breathing techniques focused on relaxation and anxiety control, which is I how I found box breathing. It was now time to cut at the root of many of my problems, which I had begun to identify as poor breathing habits.

Truthfully, in the end, the meditation recommendation was not as far off as I had previously thought. I'd encountered box breathing in other books but always under the guise or heading of meditation, and because I felt I'd already been there and done that to no avail, I dismissed it out of hand. Unfortunately, there are way too many generalizations and preconceived notions around meditation. It's almost impossible to use the word without conjuring up the scene of the Buddha sitting in the lotus position with a calm mind and the angels hovering around this perfect being who'd given up all desire so that his mind could be as reflective as clear water. It made me angry just thinking about it. But that's just me.

The idea of clearing my mind was anathema to me. Focus on the breath, breathe in, breathe out, clear your mind. Wait, did they just say focus on the breath? Yes. But I began to discern an important distinction. What they should have been saying more explicitly is focus on *how* you are breathing. And here was the Holy Grail; once you are aware of *how* you are breathing, you can change the *how* to align with *how* you want to feel. Bingo! This was the trick I had been missing, the diamond hidden in the muck that I had been searching through. It was through the practice of box breathing that I learned the important distinction between focusing on the breath and focusing on how you breathe.

So, what is box breathing?

Breath in through your nose, slow, deep, and full with your belly, to a count of four.

At the top of the breath, hold for a count of four.

Release the breath slowly to a count of four, fully hollowing out your diaphragm and abdominals.

With empty lungs, hold to a count of four.

Repeat.

That is your box 4x4x4x4. Simplicity itself. As your breathing improves you can either increase the count or slow the count. I can lose focus or possibly change cadence during the count based on which side of the box I'm doing, so to remain focused and inside the box I increase the count to five, six, etc. as my breathing improves. Another benefit of box breathing is that it can decrease total air volume intake, by lengthening the breathing pattern and decreasing the number of breaths you take in a minute. This has its own benefits which I'll get into in Chapter 7, but for now suffice it to say that just as bad breathing had negative compounding effects on my health, proper breathing had positive compounding effects.

The beauty of box breathing is that you can do it sitting, standing, walking, whatever your preference, and in just a few rounds you can feel yourself calm down. I've also found it very relaxing to do this after a workout in order to cool down and frequently use it to calm me down when I find my anxiety or anger levels rising. It works. By balancing the blood chemistry, reducing overbreathing, and decreasing the sensitivity to carbon dioxide (we will cover this in later chapters), it decreases feelings of anxiety.

This changing of the breathing pattern was the secret sauce that had been missing from my attempts at meditation. With the Wim Hof method I had learned that breathing could ready my body, wake it up, and prepare it for war. With box breathing I learned it could also calm me down when the war was over, or so that I wouldn't yell at someone when I shouldn't, or to stop my all too frequent panic attacks. When people tell you to stop and take a breath, listen. I was starting to learn that there was much wisdom in these old adages.

Box breathing and its practice also had another important side effect. Now convinced that breathing could affect how I felt, I began to pay close attention to *how* I was breathing and *how* I felt when breathing in a certain way. I began to correlate my emotional and energy states with my breath. This was another eye-opener. First, I became very aware that I was an extreme mouth breather. (Much more later on the effects and remedy for this. Hint: close your mouth and breathe through your nose.) When I could breathe, unobstructed by asthma, I gulped air. You know that person that gets on a conference call and doesn't mute, and you can hear them panting in a fashion that makes you uncomfortable? Yeah, that was me. I was now becoming aware of how I was breathing in all types of situations. The first stage of fixing something is understanding how it is broken to begin with. Becoming aware that my poor breathing patterns were at the core of my troubles gave me something to focus on, something to find a remedy for.

To start out, I suggest that the next time you find yourself angry, afraid, or stressed, pay attention to how you are breathing. Are you taking in quick, shallow breaths through your mouth? Gulping air? Hyperventilating? If so, then your breathing pattern is contributing to your emotional state, enforcing and in some cases worsening and prolonging it. Then, and here is where the miracle happened for me, change *how* you breathe. Breathe slowly through your nose. Deep breaths drawn in from your diaphragm, slow exhale out, smile. You know what I found? It was almost impossible for me to get enraged and sustain that anger when breathing in this more relaxed, natural rhythm. My heart rate would slow, that red glow would leave my face, and I could think clearly and rationally. I even applied this to other situations and was able to calm my nerves when approaching that big mountain bike jump, or before a big presentation, or to stave off shock after a bad bike crash.

As I became more and more aware of this, I noticed how breathing and the patterns of my breathing affected my emotions. Anger – quick staccato breaths followed by overbreathing and panting as I tried to catch my breath. Depressed – shallow, more inhale than exhale, with no pauses between inhale and exhale. Excited or during a workout – huge, long mouth breaths, engaging my chest, shoulders, traps and neck, gulping air with short exhales. It was all starting to click. Breathing was at the core of my emotions, my health, and my performance. And I was doing it wrong for how I wanted to feel and perform.

I could start to see the pattern. Learning how to breathe the way my body was designed to, in a way that complemented my activities and goals, had to be the primary focus of my journey to becoming a better me. Now I was convinced.

Thus far I had techniques, but as I began breathing in my box and performing the Wim Hof method I realized something important: my breathing apparatus, lungs, diaphragm, and supporting muscles were broken or weak. I had to figure out how to fix and improve their performance. Strangely enough, the key to that had nothing to do with my lungs but a little-known piece of anatomy that lay dormant in this particular asthmatic. That's what I turned to next.

Key Takeaways

- Breathing can affect our emotions and energy levels.

- Just as bad breathing can have negative compounding effects, good breathing can have positive compounding effects.

- Control how you breathe, and you can control how you feel and react.

- Box breathing is a simple technique that can reduce anxiety, anger, and aid in exercise recovery.

Core Techniques

As said before, the beauty of box breathing is that it is simple. It is best if your midsection is not cramped to get better movement from your diaphragm and breathing muscles, but you can do this sitting, standing, whatever feels comfortable, or as needed to calm down in any situation.

Take in a slow, deep nose breath initiated by your diaphragm to a count of four.

At the top of the breath pause, holding the breath for a count of four.

Let the breath out in a controlled fashion to a count of four, using diaphragmatic and abdominal controls to hollow out your midsection.

At the bottom of your exhale, pause and hold this empty-lung breath for a count of four.

This is your box 4x4x4x4. As you improve, either lengthen the time interval of your count, add a mantra, or increase the size of the box to 5x5x5x5, 6x6x6x6, etc.

At times I have also used a metronome to keep a consistent count. Metronome apps for your smartphone can be easily found for free, and I will point out where I use it for other exercises when it is difficult to use a stopwatch and you are relying on an internal count to keep time. Some find the click annoying, but I find it relaxing. To each their own.

Rinse. Wash. Repeat.

Advanced Techniques

Advanced Technique 1 – Box Breathing with Neutral Spine

For relaxation and recovery after a workout I like to use the below variation.

Lay flat on the floor. Put your arms out to your sides so that they are perpendicular with your torso. Place your calves on a chair or bench, or place your feet against a wall such that your knees are bent at a 90-degree angle, and your calves are parallel with the floor while your thighs/hamstrings are perpendicular to the floor. This creates a spine neutral position, allowing full focus on the breathing muscles and the diaphragm. Breathe in your box for at least two minutes or for as long as you want, depending on if this is in between sets/exercises, or at the end of workout, or simply to relax.

This is one of my favorites for relaxing after a long day. If you've had a rough day or a hard workout and you want to get into "calm mode" and relax for the evening, this is a great way to get there.

Advanced Technique 2 – The Long Inhale, Exhale.

This isn't a box, but I often like to start or end my box breathing with an extended inhale/exhale combination.

Breathe in as slowly and as deeply as possible for as long as possible. The goal is to lengthen the time it takes to take in a full breath, 30 seconds, a minute, etc.

At the top of the breath, go into exhale mode and try to match the inhale count. If you did 30 seconds on the inhale try to match that on the exhale, breathing out slowly using your diaphragm and abdominals to control the flow of breath, while hollowing out you midsection as you empty your lungs.

With lungs empty, I will also add in an abdominal contraction that tightens the pelvic floor muscles as I described in advanced technique variation 1 in the previous chapter. This helps to develop your pelvic floor.

I like to do breathing exercises synergistically so that all the breathing and core muscles get worked as often as possible, while also shortening the amount of time I must devote to breath-specific training.

CHAPTER 3 -
CIRCUMFERENTIAL AND
DIAPHRAGMATIC BREATHING

As far as I was concerned a diaphragm was a contraceptive. In my body it occupied the same role as my appendix. A vestigial ancient organ that served no purpose that I was aware of. Wrong, wrong, and wrong again.

I thought the diaphragm was some useless muscle that sat between my lungs and stomach. For as long as I could remember, I was an upper-chest breather. When short of breath, as I always seemed to be, I tended to breath into my upper chest, heaving up my shoulders and pulling in air with my neck muscles. If I tried to work out or had a long bout of asthma where I had to work harder to breathe, my upper back, shoulder muscles, and neck would be sore from the effort. It was a perfect demonstration of exactly the wrong way to breathe and, as you are probably beginning to see, this creates a compounding cyclic pattern where it becomes difficult to discern which came first, the chicken or the egg (the asthma or the bad breathing). Whichever was the case, the truth was that bad breathing was only working against me. As my journey continued I found that the more control I took over my breathing, working to correct it to a more natural state, the more my asthma symptoms improved. As I will continue to emphasize, that means that good patterns, corrections, and behaviors can also have a cyclic and synergistic positive effect. Small changes in my breathing, such as performing the Wim Hof method and box breathing on a daily basis, had already begun to show positive results. When I wrote about how to perform these techniques I pointed out that you should breathe from your diaphragm, through your nose; but in my journey I'd not yet gotten there. Even when performing these techniques, I was doing it with open mouth using my upper chest to pull air into my lungs. That was not optimal, and it was about to change.

Up till this point I was performing breathing exercises that focused on getting more air into my lungs (Wim Hof method) or slowed my breathing volume and pace (box breathing). Both had helped me immensely but neither corrected my bad breathing habits. Habits I wasn't aware that I had. Nor did I know that they were bad. What I was about to learn was that my breathing muscles, the real breathing muscles, were not being utilized and that I had to change how I breathed and with which muscles. This chapter and the next will focus on the fundamental changes I had to make in order to improve my moment-by-moment breathing. And this started with learning to breathe with my diaphragm.

Why is it that many people do not breathe through their diaphragms naturally or utilize the full scope and power of their diaphragms? There are a lot of speculations. We spend most of our sedentary lives sitting behind desks, hunched over with poor posture, staring at screens, and this position contracts and puts pressure on our primary breathing muscles (the diaphragm). Therefore, we resort to upper-chest breathing, which is called a vertical breath because we draw air into our lungs using our chest, neck, and shoulders. There is also the vanity hypothesis, that breathing through our diaphragms is not sexy, as a healthy diaphragm when expanded will enlarge the midsection and expand the belly and rib cage on inhales. When you breathe vertically, you pull your stomach in, recreating that slim-waisted superhero look. Observing athletes, it seemed like many of them were breathing with their chests and pulling their stomachs in. If professional athletes were chest breathing, how could it be wrong? These were the cardio beasts that I hoped to become. The truth, however, is that this type of vertical breathing is suboptimal at best.

Whatever the reason is for how we ended up here, I for one was not using my diaphragm properly. As I was to learn, it was not some small slice of muscle below the lungs but a large muscle that went entirely around the inside of my ribs and strengthened my torso when inflated (see Figure 1 showing the position of the diaphragm). As a muscle it could be used to inflate the lungs from the bottom up. If you look at the shape of the lungs, the bottom has a larger surface area with a denser clustering of blood vessels for absorbing oxygen (see Figure 2). As I will explain later, not only does increasing the strength and endurance of your diaphragm drastically improve breathing efficiency, it also stabilizes the torso, spine, and connects with the pelvic floor to link the upper and lower torso together. By inflating this muscle to push against the walls of our ribs and abdomen, our torso is given stability for activities like powerlifting; or deflating it which gives us improved rotation and flexibility, as when performing yoga movements. The ability to breathe properly and maintain tension in your core is important in strength training. Using the diaphragm braces your body by creating intrathoracic and intra-abdominal pressure, which stabilizes and strengthens your core.

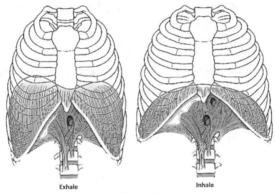

Exhale   Inhale

Figure 1. Diaphragm Anatomy

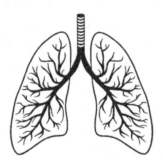

Figure 2. Lung Diagram

As I discovered during my own training, my inability to maintain this pressure during lifts caused injury and became a limiting factor in my performance. My core was giving out way before my legs or other muscles. Not to mention that the ability to properly breathe will also balance your blood chemistry (oxygen/carbon dioxide (CO_2) levels), which supplies you with the energy you need to complete these lifts in the first place. Understanding how to coordinate my breath with the inflation and deflation of my diaphragm to add either strength or flexibility became a very powerful tool in my journey towards becoming a badass.

With all that said, when I started this my diaphragm was about as useful as an appendix; I thought it was one of those biological fossils that would in time just disappear during the course of evolution. When I learned its function and how to use it, I realized how wrong I was.

Let's pause for a moment and count the ways that we are currently aware of in which I was breathing incorrectly: short, gasping breaths, always through my mouth – check; using chest, shoulder, and neck muscles to pull air into my lungs – check; filling up only the top of the lungs instead of the more expansive and alveoli-dense lower lung (the place where oxygen and carbon dioxide are exchanged between the lungs and blood during respiration) –check. So, I was an upper-chest, mouth breather. Yahtzee.

If you were to look at a picture of the lungs, you'd notice one obvious thing: they are larger at the bottom than at the top (See Figure 2 above). And why would that be? That design doesn't make sense if we are breathing through our chests. You may also notice that the density of blood vessels that carry the products of breathing to the rest of the body (the alveoli) are more plentiful here as well. This seems like an obviously faulty design if we are breathing incorrectly, but transforming air into energy doesn't end with the lungs. The missing link in this breathing alchemy is the diaphragm, which turns this anatomical picture upside down. The lungs are not muscles; therefore, we need to use primary and ancillary muscles to move air in and out of our lungs. When performing a vertical breath, you are using your chest, trapezius, and neck muscles to breathe (these are ancillary breathing muscles). Not only are you breathing inefficiently with this method, but you are taxing those muscles just to supply your body with oxygen. Meanwhile, you are not utilizing the primary breathing muscle, your diaphragm, which was purpose-built for this. If you look at its anatomical structure, it relieves the pressure from your ancillary muscles so they don't have to put more effort into breathing while also supporting your core. All this just by breathing properly. It turns out, this is a perfect design (see Figures 1 & 2).

Try this. Run around, do jumping jacks, burpees, whatever, until you have to take deeper breaths or feel you are running out of air. Now stand up straight and look at your reflection in a mirror. Are your shoulders moving? Your chest? As you try to catch your breath, does it look like you are doing a set of shrugs? Does your stomach tuck into your rib cage as you breathe in, giving you that nice, slim, svelte, athletic look? These are all sign of inefficient vertical breathing. Paradoxically, the cardio-monster is described as a barrel-chested warrior with six-pack abs that could blow the roof off a house. In truth, the badass breather has a wide midsection with a bulging rib cage supporting a horizontal breath. This allows for 360-degree (circumferential) breathing with the diaphragm, which, once strong, will increase muscular and cardiovascular endurance.

Why is this muscle so important and what was the role it played in my journey of breath?

First, when you use your diaphragm, breathing massages your internal organs, liver, kidneys, stomach, and intestines, allowing them to function better. The widening and narrowing of the middle of your body during expansion and relaxation of the diaphragm enhances circulation, digestion, and the movement of lymph. These benefits then expand to include controlling aspects of the sympathetic and parasympathetic nervous system, which govern the body's arousal level through the release of neurotransmitters that determine stress and relaxation responses. Use of the diaphragm also allows for better control of the volume and pace of breathing which, as we will learn in Chapter 7, gives you greater control over your state of mental and physical arousal from completely relaxed, to ready for war, and everything in between.

Second, by using the diaphragm you can expand the amount of air that can be pushed into the lungs, and you can also control what part of the lungs you breathe with. This will become important later when we look at advanced breathing techniques which are important for athletes looking to optimize oxygen intake even when their bodies are not in the optimal position for traditional horizontal breathing, such as when biking, climbing, grappling, engaging in jujitsu, or wearing a weighted vest or powerlifting support belt.

Third, and this was the key for me, the diaphragm can be used to stabilize your core. If you expand and contract your diaphragm, coordinating it with your physical movements and needs, you not only give yourself a breathing advantage but a core strength and flexibility advantage as mentioned above. For me this became a huge help in powerlifting exercises like the squat and deadlift.

As a young man, when my asthma interfered with me building up my cardiorespiratory capacity, I looked for sports that didn't require great lung capacity and turned to powerlifting. I loved lifting heavy weights. At a body weight of 230 lbs. and with no suit or wraps, I had a deadlift of 605 lbs. and a squat of 585 lbs. As I will continue to point out during the course of this book, not breathing properly ended my powerlifting hobby as well. I did not have great form, never had a trainer, and had injured my lower back multiple times both in the squat and deadlift. My last day of heavy lifting ended when, during a 600 lbs. squat attempt, my back completely folded. Two hours later I had to crawl on hands and knees into my house from the car. If not for being in a squat rack with a spotter that prevented me from impacting with the floor, things could have been much worse. Even so, for over a week I walked around as if I had a stick up my ass, unable to bend over or sleep without pain. I was done. I was 32 years old. I told myself that my body just wasn't built for heavy weights. It was then that I started to believe that maybe my body wasn't built for any of the physical activities that I wanted to engage in.

Years later I wanted to try it again, believing that if I started light and worked my way up slowly I could develop my back and spine to be able to handle heavy loads again. Even with weights of 185lbs. for squats and 135 lbs. for deadlift I felt that tightness in my back. I was very discouraged. Then I found the beauty and power of filling my diaphragm to support my torso, knitting together the muscles of my abdomen, spine, and pelvis to increase stability. If you remember the anatomical makeup of the diaphragm and its placement in the body (see Figure 1 above), it wraps around your core inside your ribs. Once filled it creates pressure within your midsection that links the abdominal muscles with the back and spine, strengthening them. Imagine wearing a weight belt around your waist but when you squat down you suck in your gut while breathing in. What happens? The support belt loosens, which is the exact opposite of what it is supposed to do. When wearing a support belt, you should be breathing into it, making it tighter so it can add support. The muscles of the torso, when linked with proper breathing and the expansion of the diaphragm can do this naturally; the belt, if needed to help stabilization during heavier weights, is meant to take advantage of this breathing pattern and multiply its effects. If done wrong it provides little aid and can actually work against you by giving you just enough support to allow you to perform the activity with bad form and bad breathing. With that technique you will never reach your full potential.

In the past I did tons of core work in an attempt to make my lower back stronger, because that was what I read was the key to improving lower back strength. That came to no avail because I wasn't linking those muscles to the back to stabilize it. The advice to strengthen the core was not incorrect; I was just missing the important point of linking all these stronger muscles together via the breath to add stability. When I knew how to use my diaphragm, I could. The trick was filling my diaphragm as I sat (lowered) into the squat or deadlift. That pressure was like using a power suit and weight belt combined, linking all the core stabilizer muscles into a synergistic whole. I would then hold the breath and pressure at the lower position. As I pushed upward I would let out little whiffs of air if necessary. At the top of the move, I would then take in a further puff of air making sure that my core stayed tight, never contracting my diaphragm while under load, breathing in and out only what was necessary to continue the movements without ever fully deflating and hollowing out my midsection until the weight was racked again. This had the added benefit of including some short breath holds into the exercise to increase carbon dioxide resistance and improve anaerobic and aerobic performance.

A pattern for breathing and when to inflate/deflate your diaphragm can then be developed for any movement or exercise based on when you need stability versus flexibility. When the diaphragm deflates and the midsection hollows out, this allows for better rotation and contraction of the torso. You can benefit from these breathing patterns when dancing, doing martial arts, or practicing yoga, using the stability/flexibility paradigm to determine when to inflate and deflate. In some cases, it also may be beneficial to create a semi-static or neutral diaphragm state, using a combination of holds and short puffs of breath to maintain stability. This type of pattern can maintain core stability while allowing for quick breaths during longer exercises where the body is constantly under strain, such as in the squat and deadlift for repetitions, or when carrying heavier weights over distance, such as in a sandbag/rock carry or the farmer's walk. These exercises help develop patterns of breathing that support core stability over the course of longer duration exercises.

As I explored diaphragmatic breathing I learned to quickly expand and contract my diaphragm for more advanced movement, linking my breath, core stability, and movement. I'll cover this topic in more depth in Chapter 6 when I explain the Systema exercises that I incorporated into my routines. The key takeaway from this chapter is that the diaphragm is the primary breathing muscle and, if used and manipulated in coordination with physical movement, provides a one-two punch that can have a profound effect on your strength due to the added core stability while also making breathing more efficient, putting less strain on your body by properly feeding it with the needed oxygen levels during exercise. All of this improves performance and makes you less prone to certain types of injuries. So, get the glossy magazine cover superhero image with a thin waist, pulled-in abdominals, and a puffed-out chest out of your head. Instead focus on strength, function, and stability, and start breathing circumferentially with your diaphragm.

Bottom line, if you want to become optimal you must learn to breath circumferentially. As soon as your breathing suffers and your body feels it is becoming oxygen starved, it focuses more of its resources on pulling in more oxygen, overtaxing the lungs, heart, and all the muscles that support drawing in more air. As a result, there is an increase of lactic acid concentrations in the muscles, resulting in muscular fatigue and a feeling of heaviness and searing pain. Optimize your breathing, and your muscles will be rewarded with increased strength, endurance, and the ability to quickly recover. In addition, optimized oxygen consumption and breathing results in better cognitive performance, especially under physically stressful activities, which can further increase performance and flow.

Circumferential breathing with the diaphragm was one of the most important discoveries on this journey to badass breathing. This knowledge, combined with what we will discuss in the next chapter, fully ignited my hidden abilities. Till now I'd improved my asthma. I could lift weights again. I could ride my mountain bike without using my inhaler. With a horizontal, circumferential breathing pattern I felt like I was getting more oxygen, but I was still laboring. I felt like I had to work harder to breathe than anyone else I biked or worked out with. This was frustrating given all the effort I was putting in. The people I biked with didn't work out like I did. They weren't running or lifting weights during the week, but I was still gasping at the top of the hill whereas they were only slightly out of breath. Why? Was it truly that my asthma had permanently damaged my lungs and I began too far behind the starting line to catch up? That is what I believed until I found that crucial piece of the puzzle which linked together all the work I'd done up till this point and made me a breathing badass!

Key Takeaways

- The diaphragm is your primary breathing muscle and should be used as such. When used properly it fills the lungs in an anatomically efficient way from the bottom up, where the largest lung volume and capillaries are for delivering oxygen to your blood and organs.

- The diaphragm is a stabilizer of the core and, when inflated and linked with the muscles of the abdomen and pelvis, provides superior stabilization for lifting, running, and other physical activities.

- Linking diaphragm inflation and deflation will free your body to use energy to fuel muscles rather than oxygen intake, improving athletic performance. It will also improve stability and flexibility within your core.

Core Techniques

First we must start by expanding that which is currently caging the diaphragm, the ribs and the muscles of the core and midsection. There are a lot of exercises that will do this, but I have two that provided the most benefits. Once you start applying diaphragm breathing to movements, you will begin to understand that all movements done in coordination with the breath and diaphragm will help you expand your breathing apparatus, making it stronger and more efficient.

First we will focus on expanding the ribs and muscles that may be constraining the expansion of the diaphragm and then turn to strengthening the diaphragm itself.

The Dead-Hang Circumferential Breath

The dead hang is one of my favorite exercises because it has a number of benefits, including the stretching of the tendons and ligaments of the shoulder, while also improving grip strength and endurance. For the purposes of optimizing our breathing, it helps to expand the ribs and stretch the musculature around the midsection.

With hands shoulder-width apart, hang from a bar with your legs dangling. Now it's time to expand the diaphragm; start with a few small breaths and then gradually inhale more and more into the diaphragm with each successive breath. Because the midsection is stretched by gravity, the expansion and relaxation of the diaphragm will increase the stretch of the abdominal muscles and the ribs. Focus on stretching and expanding the ribs and musculature. Become more aware with each breath of how your diaphragm is moving; consciously expand it outward 360 degrees around your torso, pushing against the ribs, the abdominal wall, and the muscles of the back. This is the good spare tire you have been missing. You want to expand outward, giving your diaphragm more room so that it can work more efficiently and doesn't have to fight against the constraints of muscle, tissue, and bone.

The Overhead Pull

The second exercise is the overhead pull. Using a dumbbell, kettle-bell, or other weight, lay across (perpendicular) a flat bench such that your shoulders are on the edge of the surface with your head dangling over the edge (see Figure 3). The surface should be stable such that there is no risk of it toppling over during the exercise. It also must be far enough off the ground such that your arms can go behind your head and down (see Figure 3), allowing you to stretch your midsection. Grab the weight from the ground and, with elbows in, pull it over your head till it is perpendicular to your chest. With elbows in and slightly bent, lower the weight back towards the ground behind your head. Take a breath in as you do so, expanding your ribs and midsection. As the weight approaches the ground, breathe in as deeply as you can under tension. Then begin to breath out slowly, hollowing out your midsection as you bring the weight back to perpendicular over your chest.

Figure 3 – The Overhead Pull

Use very light weights to start. This is not a weight-lifting exercise but a midsection-expansion exercise. Always remember the goal. Only use as much weight as is needed to create a stretch and feel those bones and muscles expanding under the load as you breathe in deep with your diaphragm at the bottom of the movement. As with any stretch, don't overdo it. If it feels uncomfortable, back off. For the first rep, take more shallow breaths. Increase the depth of the breath with each successive rep. Keep the weight light doing two to three sets with seven to 10 repetitions per set. Again, this should be considered more of a stretch than a muscle exercise, so treat it as such.

This same type of breathing can be used in any position in which you are expanding your chest, like yoga moves, back bends, etc. Once you understand how it feels you'll easily be able to apply the pattern to other exercises. Then you can see how to apply it to other movements, paying attention to when you need an expanded diaphragm strengthening and stiffening your core while linking your abdominal muscles, spine, and pelvic floor; and when you need the flexibility of an empty diaphragm, hollowing out the midsection allowing for more rotation, bending, etc.

Trampoline Jumping

One of my favorite training tools for learning to properly breathe and add support to my movement via the diaphragm is the trampoline. To have a stable midsection during jumps, you quickly expand your core on impact and then maintain core stability and strength by taking small breaths or sips of air. If you then perform some type of gymnastics move, like a flip, you will have to quickly hollow out your midsection in order to gain flexibility, followed by a filling of the diaphragm to provide stability back to your core on impact.

Trampolines are also good at highlighting when you are not linking your core to your pelvic floor. When you are jumping straight up and down, your hips and torso will stay locked. The downward pressure of landing on the trampoline before getting ready to jump again will make your pelvic floor feel "loose" if you are not breathing into it and locking it with your core muscles via the diaphragm. Without going into too much detail, if you feel like you have to use the restroom after jumping for a while, you may not be properly stabilizing your pelvic floor. The trampoline allows you to take a rapid but simple movement which enables you to focus on the type of breathing that works. Once you understand the framework and how to use your breath and push it to different areas of your body, you can apply this learning to movements and activities like running and martial arts. This will require more advanced, fast-paced expansion and contraction of the diaphragm to link your movements with breath; but, with a strong base and feel for how to use the breath, it will become more intuitive. Using tools like trampoline jumps can help to create this strong base.

Strengthening Your Diaphragm and Learning to Breathe Circumferentially

Now we can focus on increasing the strength and endurance of the diaphragm while learning to breathe using different quadrants of the diaphragm.

Breathe in through your nose, inflating your diaphragm, and then slowly release allowing your diaphragm to hollow out your midsection. As you breathe try to increase the expansion of your diaphragm, not just in your belly but around your entire midsection. Feel the air pushing outward against your ribs, your sides, then your back. Once you get the hang of this circumferential breathing, feel it link with the pelvic muscles with each breath, adding stability and flexibility to your pelvic floor on inhales and exhales.

Pay attention to how you breathe. Especially if you work at a desk where your midsection may be compressed. Maintain good posture to reduce stress on your body and make it more natural to breathe through your diaphragm. Use a stand-up desk or simply make sure you get up often. Even when sitting you should be breathing with your diaphragm. Till this became natural for me, I would set an alert on my phone or a reminder on my laptop. I started with an alert every 15 minute and gradually increased the time interval as it became more natural to breathe in this manner. At these times I would check in with my breathing to make sure I was using my diaphragm and breathing slowly through my nose.

In addition, be conscious of how you are breathing while moving and exercising. Not just that you are using your diaphragm but your pattern of breathing and your pace. Begin controlling into which of the various quadrants of your diaphragm and lungs you breathe. As an example, if you are bent over, as you would be on a bicycle, push more air into your back and sides as opposed to your abdomen. If your back and stomach are constrained, as they would be with a weighted vest or plate carrier, breathe into the sides of your ribs.

A good way to practice this is to place your palms on the areas you want to push air into and get them to move. Belly, sides, ribs, back. Move them higher, lower, always trying to get air into that area so you can feel your body pushing against your palms. This is a great exercise, and you will be amazed at how much control you really have as to where you breathe from and how you can get a full breath even when part of your body is constrained. At Spartan races, there is a bucket carry where the bucket is pushing against your stomach, making it difficult to breathe from the abdomen. This was a perfect tool for teaching me how to breathe from the ribs and back, which is also useful for a lot of strongman-type lifts and carries that constrict belly breathing.

Advanced Techniques

Advanced Technique 1 – Diaphragm Lunge and Twist

This will look very similar to a modified "warrior one" yoga pose (see Figure 4). Put your right foot out, toes pointed forward, and put your left foot behind you in a lunge-ready position. Unlike with warrior one, your rear toes go to the ground facing the same direction as your front foot. As you let your midsection move towards the ground in a controlled fashion, take a deep breath in and keep your torso upright while your front calf is perpendicular with the floor and your knee is at 90 degrees or less as you allow your body to sink. Do not let your rear knee touch the floor. We want this to stretch. Raise your hands from your sides till they are directly overhead and raise your chin to look up at your hands. Bend your back slightly, arching it at the middle. Take in a few deep belly breaths, feeling the expansion of your ribs.

Figure 4 – The Diaphragm Lunge and Twist (back bend)

Now bring your torso upright and perpendicular to the floor again and twist your hips. Face in the direction of whatever leg is forward. In this case, because your right foot is forward, you will twist to the right. Twist to the point where your eyes can focus on something perpendicular to your body. Hollow out your midsection by releasing your breath and twist further. Hold for a few seconds and then slowly come back to facing forward (see Figure 5). Slowly come back up to a standing position, and then repeat with the other leg forward.

Figure 5 – The Diaphragm Lunge and Twist (the twist)

This is a great exercise for expanding the ribs and stretching the spine, back, and pelvic muscles while also showing the effectiveness of coordinating movement with breathing patterns.

Advanced Technique 2 – The Heel Grab Back Bend

This is not for everyone. Sit on your heels with your knees pointed slightly outward. Grab your heels with your hands and then slowly start to rise to your knees while arching your back, pushing your pelvis forward while holding onto your heels for balance. Push your pelvis further forward, bend your back, and let your head fall backward. This looks like a backbend but with you holding your heels (see Figure 6)

Figure 6 – The Heel Grab Back Bend

Keep your eyes open, as closing them can make you feel dizzy. This is one exercise where I will use my mouth to breathe, because I want to take in quick, deep bursts. Breathe into the belly using your mouth and concentrate on expanding the diaphragm. Take in short, quick, deep breaths trying to pull in as much air as quickly as you can. Stretch and expand as you pull the air in. Let it out in a rush, pursing your lips and forcing the air out. This breath should be quick enough that it makes a hissing sound. Repeat for four or five breaths, and then ease back down to the starting position with your butt on your heels. To start, do one or two sets, and then work your way up to four or five. This exercise expands your rib cage and allows you to quickly fill and release your diaphragm.

Advanced Technique 3 – The Exhale Count

This one is all about diaphragm control. Take in a deep breath through your nose and, as you let the breath out, begin to count out loud. The goal here is to get to as high a count as possible, slowly controlling the contraction of your diaphragm to lengthen the exhale and extend the amount of breath you have for the count. Start by counting at a normal speaking volume, and try to slowly release the air from your diaphragm. As you begin to run out of air, lower the volume till you can only whisper. Once you can no longer even whisper, move your lips to continue the count even when it seems there is nothing left. Keep counting with your lips, trying to push out little sips of air. Hollow out your midsection as you strive to get out one more number.

Once you can no longer force any more air out, prepare to take a controlled breath in. Control the breath, and breathe in as slowly as possible. Take a few slow, deep breaths in and out, breathe normally for a minute, and then do the exercise again. Do three or four rounds.

This exercise increases the strength of the diaphragm and the exhale muscles, allowing you to control not only inhalation, exhalation and inflation, deflation of the diaphragm but also the speed at which this occurs. This is an exercise used by vocal instructors to train singers to control the output of their voice for those longer notes and then quickly recover. If you are a singer, then using this exercise combined with other vocal exercises will work synergistically.

CHAPTER 4 - THE NOSE KNOWS

This entire journey in breath had many twists and turns. Also, I did not learn the most important lessons early on. Everything I learned on this journey played a role in making me an asthma-free, badass breather, but none, and I mean none, had the impact of simply switching to breathing through my nose.

Do I wish I had learned this important lesson first and saved myself a lot of frustration? Maybe. However, I also realize that I may not have been motivated to explore and research other techniques if my journey had started here. Breathing through my nose may have made me asthma free, although I don't know this for sure, but it would not have made me a badass breathing warrior. For that I would need to incorporate all the techniques covered in this book. Strangely enough, during my research I'd not seen nose breathing, diaphragm breathing, and many of the techniques I detail here covered in great depth. Most sources tended to focus on a favored element of breathing, claiming it to be the most important. I'd seen mention of nose breathing when talking about certain exercises, yoga, or meditation techniques, but it was presented as a tangential suggestion rather than something that was critical to the performance of the exercise itself. So, for example, breathing through the nose and out through the mouth would be recommended, but the focus was on the technique itself (the pace or count of the breath, the mental image to focus on, etc.) not on the importance of breathing through the nose while performing the exercise. I'd yet to see a reference that put the importance of nose breathing front and center. In addition, I had not heard of the importance of breathing through the nose all the time. My focus had been on breathwork. Learning about diaphragmatic breathing had introduced me to the fact that my everyday breathing was broken and needed to be fixed. I had developed a badass diaphragm and was regularly using it as my primary breathing muscle, but I was still breathing exclusively through my mouth. This too needed to be corrected.

Nose breathing and diaphragm breathing are corrections. Our modern dysfunctional breathing has led to a need to retrain ourselves to breathe the way we were born to, the way our ancestors did – closed mouthed, using our diaphragms. Modern, sedentary life has changed the way we breathe. I had been living under the assumption that because breathing is automatic our bodies know what to do and do it correctly. Truth is our modern lifestyles have turned us into gasping mouth breathers. We over-breathe, resulting in an imbalance in blood chemistry so that no matter how much we breathe, we feel air hunger. Just like with the modern American diet where we are starving ourselves of the nutrients we need by overeating empty calories that do nothing for the body, we are starving ourselves of the right oxygen levels with improper breathing – and it all starts with the nose. The nose knows.

To become badass breathers, we must start by going back to doing what is natural, what our bodies were designed to do, and then add some age-old exercises, performance science, and breathwork. The combination of nose breathing and diaphragm breathing alone will change your life. If you leave this book with nothing else, leave with that.

To close the loop on my regret for not starting here, someone once told me that if you are happy with where you are in life, you have to accept and be at peace with everything that got you there, good and bad. So, at the end of the day, the answer is no, I don't regret having taken the convoluted path I have; it's what brought me here, writing this book, and hopefully sharing some useful knowledge with others that can benefit from it.

But before we get into the amazing benefits, let's just briefly take a look at the nose and why it's so important.

- Filters and warms the air we breathe.

- Releases nitric oxide, which is a vasodilator, increasing blood vessel dilation, and triggering oxygen absorption which produces a synergistic effect for increasing oxygen availability to our organs and muscles.

- Regulates intake of air, which prevents overbreathing (a condition common when habitually mouth breathing). Overbreathing reduces the levels of carbon dioxide (CO_2) present in the blood, creating CO_2 sensitivity resulting in a feeling of air hunger. Increased levels of CO_2 is also a chemical trigger for red blood cells to absorb more oxygen. If these levels do not rise, due to the combined effects of overbreathing and CO_2 sensitivity, oxygen absorption will be suboptimal. In addition, if CO_2 levels do not rise, hemoglobin (the iron-rich protein that binds oxygen and CO_2 in red blood cells) may not release the oxygen molecules they have currently bound. This results in a further decline in overall oxygen availability.

As I pointed out in previous chapters, I'd come a long way but seemed to be missing some essential ingredient because my cardio did not seem to ever reach the level of amateur athlete, even though I was expending a significant amount of time and effort training. It turned out that nose breathing was the missing link. Once I trained myself to nose breathe, it immediately ignited my cardio and had a compounding effect when combined with all the other lessons I'd learned thus far, especially diaphragm breathing and the Wim Hof method. It was also the basis for exploring more advanced techniques and training regimens I'll describe in later chapters. Without the incorporation of the nose, the journey would have ended in good but not great, baseline but not badass; and good was not where I was struggling to get to.

What I found strange is that not many people were talking about the importance of breathing through the nose. I'd been to a host of pulmonary specialists throughout my life and not one had ever asked if I breathed through my nose or told me I should start doing so. Even breath warriors like Wim Hof never highlighted its importance, at least not in the material I'd reviewed. Again, it may be mentioned as part of a particular breathing exercise, but as a general rule for everyday breathing I'd not seen it emphasized until I read James Nestor's book *Breath: The New Science of a Lost Art*. Once I knew what I was looking for and its importance, I found more and more references; but again, it did not seem as prevalent as breathing techniques and meditation. My only theory for this is that it is boring and aside from encouraging people to breathe through their nose all or most of the time, there was not a lot more left to say. End of lesson. And to some extent that is true; but without going into a little more depth, many may not understand how important nose breathing is and why.

Up till this point I was an extreme mouth breather. I never breathed through my nose. Even when eating or drinking I was the guy holding his breath or breathing around his food while he ate. Disgusting, right? I just felt like I could never get enough air, and the truth was that because I was not breathing through my nose, my body was not absorbing the oxygen I was breathing. It was a vicious, self-defeating cycle. I was overbreathing, putting greater demands and stress on my breathing apparatus (diaphragm, lungs, and ancillary muscles). I was dehydrating faster by expending more moisture through an open mouth (which also contributes to gum disease, tooth decay, bad breath, and dry mouth/throat). I was increasing the amount of bacteria that went into my mouth and potentially into my lungs because it was not being filtered by the nose and septum. All of which was contributing to my asthma and allergies because the air I was breathing was unfiltered.

The first step, boring as it is, was to be conscious of my breathing and ensure that, as often as possible, I was breathing through my nose until it became a habit. I particularly focused on this while working out and biking. Here you may have to put your ego to one side, as I did. I could not keep up my usual pace, rep count, milage, with pure nose breathing when I first started. The body needs time to adjust. I told myself during these activities that the focus needed to be on breathing through my nose and using my diaphragm, not on getting my best lap time or rep count. I needed to believe that the returns down the road would be worth it. And believe me, they are. The body needs time, and I implore you to give it that time; it will reward you in many ways. The results for me, after just one month, were amazing.

Mountain bike climbs, which would normally have me gasping for breath, I was doing with a normal breathing cycle through the nose. And the fact that I was breathing less but absorbing more oxygen meant that my breathing muscles were not working as hard. I was getting more oxygen to my muscles and organs and, as a result, had much better cardio and muscular endurance. That 10-mile ride that I thought I was going to have to give up before starting on this journey became little more than a warm up.

There will be causes and times to engage in mouth breathing, as we will explore later, but for the most part I would complete 90% of a bike ride or workout without having to open my mouth. Therefore, in my experience, once you engage the nose, the reasons to mouth breathe will be few and far between; but when you do mouth breathe, you'll know it was the right thing to do because it is like engaging another gear and putting your body into overdrive. When you nose breathe you get the release of nitric oxide causing vasodilation, which means a larger pipe for the blood to travel through. Then you get the increased CO_2 levels, which triggers further oxygen absorption and release of oxygen by hemoglobin. If you then add mouth breathing and suck in more oxygen after these biological triggers have been pulled, your body is ready to absorb and use that increased oxygen. Without ramping things up like this, pulling in more oxygen via the mouth is nothing more than a means of putting more stress on the breathing musculature and increasing sensitivity to CO_2, all resulting in a feeling of air hunger. Even on exercises that require quick, deep breaths to fill the diaphragm, such as squats or deadlifts, I found that nose breathing increased my strength and stamina.

Once you switch over to habitual nose breathing you can experiment with when and where to get the benefits of occasional mouth breathing, but to start I suggest a mouth-breathing hiatus. Otherwise, you will find yourself subconsciously switching back to mouth breathing. You will also more quickly train your body to deal with less air and decrease your sensitivity to CO2. This has a lot of health benefits in and of itself, some of which I've already mentioned like increased oxygen absorption, but also increased resistance to pain, increasing the time it takes to build up lactic acid (a byproduct of muscular contraction that causes the burn, which quickly turns into the heavy feeling in your limbs), increased tolerance to stress, which contributes to fewer panic attacks and less anxiety and depression.

For those times when I wasn't conscious (sleeping) or during activities where I found myself mouth breathing without realizing it (e.g., hiking), I resorted to medical tape to keep my lips closed until the habit formed and I no longer needed it. For sleeping this was an absolute necessity. If you wake up with bad breath, dry mouth, or you snore, you are mouth breathing while you sleep. There are lots of mouth tapes available to buy online. I use 3M Micropore tape in the center of my lips. It has a light adhesive, which I don't press to the lips but on the skin directly above and below my lips. This slight tension seems to do the trick. Performing a BOLT score test upon waking will also let you know if you are nose breathing during sleep. Your BOLT score should increase by two to five seconds after only a few weeks of using tape, as mine did (see how to perform the BOLT test in the assessment section at the beginning of the book). This may seem like a crazy idea, but it works.

For hiking I used a training mask (more on masks in Chapter 8) because it made me more aware of my breathing, which is all I needed to switch to nose breathing and make it a habit. For some reason it was easy for me to be aware of my breathing when biking, lifting, and more rigorous exercising. I theorized that because I needed to control my breathing during these exercises I was more conscious of how I was breathing, whereas hiking was my Zen activity and I wasn't focused on my breathing. If there is a specific activity where you find it difficult to notice that you have switched to mouth breathing, then I suggest tape or some other means of increasing breath awareness during that activity.

You want another good reason for nose breathing and mouth taping? At times my wife had to sleep in another room because my snoring would wake her up or keep her from falling asleep. Even my children, sleeping a fair distance down the hall with multiple closed doors to shield the noise, would complain that I would wake them up. They were the first beneficiaries of my nose breathing. But I was also sleeping better and feeling more rested upon waking. After two weeks of nose breathing and tape – No snoring. No complaints. Happy wife, happy life.

The body is habitual and, even now, especially if I have a semi-clogged nose (which also happens much less frequently), I will open my mouth during sleep and snore. If that happens I go right back to the tape.

The tape works. Make sure you use a low-adhesive tape that does not damage your skin or lips when you remove it, and do not use if you are feeling sick or nauseous when you go to bed. Another trick is to place a few drops of olive oil, avocado oil, or other edible oil on your lips aligned with the area you are going to tape. This allows the tape to stick to the skin above and below and avoids damaging the more sensitive skin of your lips. As I said, in two weeks I saw the benefits. I used tape consistently for a month and then would use it only for the occasional re-training if needed. As of this writing, I have not used tape in more than six months.

There you have it. By adding the nose to my breathing, I was finally functioning like an amateur athlete. Mountain-biking friends that I had previously had a hard time keeping up with I was now outperforming, and I went from the top 20% in the open class of Spartan finishers to consistently being in the top 10% by changing nothing more than which orifice I breathed through. The nose really does know.

But my journey was not yet complete. I had been restored to baseline, breathing the way our bodies were made to breathe. I had corrected my asthma, my snoring, and was breathing circumferentially with my diaphragm; but I still had a few lessons to learn before I became a badass breather. The truth is that becoming badass is an ever-evolving process, as are all journeys of discovery. It's a constant cycle of challenge, growth, and improvement. The journey never ends. Let's explore what came next.

Key Takeaways

- Breathe through your nose. Period. Or at least get started on making the switch. If you have allergies, are congested, breathe as often as you can with your nose. The more I forced myself to breathe through the nose, the clearer that passage seemed to get. If you don't use it, you will lose it; and I found the more I used it, the more useful it became. If you have to start slow, no problem. Just start.

- The nose and septum filter the air you breathe, resulting in fewer toxins, bacteria, and viruses making it to your lungs.

- Breathing through your nose releases nitric oxide, which expands the highways through which your blood travels, the blood vessels. In addition, the lower volume of breathing will increase levels of CO_2, triggering the absorption of oxygen while simultaneously releasing the oxygen trapped in hemoglobin. This means your breathing muscles can pull in less volume of air to fuel your body, making your entire physiology more efficient.

- Bottom line: Breathing through your nose has the power to unlock your full badass potential.

Core Technique

Close your mouth, breathe through your nose.

For sleeping, use mouth tape. Breathe through your nose.

Did I mention you should breathe through your nose?

Advanced Techniques

Advanced Technique 1 – Nose Humming

Close your mouth and hum a tune through your nose. These vibrations cause sensors in your nasal cavity to trigger the release of nitric oxide, which can increase vasodilation and oxygen absorption. I like to do this while warming up for exercise as it gets my body primed for absorbing more oxygen once I start going full tilt.

CHAPTER 5 - EMBODIED BREATHING — A MOMENT OF REFLECTION

If you've been following along on the journey thus far, you may have come to realize a few things. Breathing, as modern humans, is not as simple as pulling air into our lungs by any method possible and then exhaling it. You can survive that way, but not thrive. Whatever it was that led us to breathe in an inefficient way, the fact is that it is not the way our bodies were meant to breathe. To realize our full physical, mental, and spiritual potential we must start with correcting how we breathe.

If you have practiced some of the techniques in the preceding chapters of this book, then you have learned that controlling how you breathe can control your energy levels, from relaxed (box breathing) to energized (Wim Hof method); and correcting improper breathing can lead to increased physical and mental performance and improved overall well-being and health. In the next chapter we will get into more advanced training techniques to manipulate breathing to turn you into a badass breathing warrior; but for now, we realize that even though breathing is simply an environmental and biological exchange of gases and chemicals, we can manipulate this alchemical process and control how our bodies respond to it.

Let us pause there to truly embody that process. Our bodies have evolved to interface directly with the environment around us, to transform air into energy. This amazing physiological process works in conjunction with the environment to create life, movement, and change.

At the risk of sounding hokey, it is the breath that puts us most in touch with our world and ourselves. With each breath we transmute the blessings of the air into life-giving energy, which we then use to transform the world we live in. The engine of life is not just within us; it is a collaboration. Our insides turned outside, and vice versa, as we take the external in, transform it, and then breathe out. It is a process that connects us to the environment that surrounds us. Nowhere is the relationship between us and our planet more intimate and immediate.

I have come from a place where I was sure that my life was measured in how many breaths I had left in my body. This is true for all of us, but I was acutely aware of it because of my asthma. If we take no breath for granted, then we should want to take every breath in such a way that it blesses our bodies and primes us for the task at hand, however great or small. That is how we were built; to use that blessing to achieve great things and positively transform our world. To not do this is to squander an evolutionary gift.

On this journey we've come to realize that we can breathe more fully by using our diaphragms. Our diaphragms can, in turn, be used to strengthen our core and be deflated to allow for greater fluidity and flexibility. Controlling the rate and depth of our breathing can enable control of our emotions instead of being controlled by them. We can modify heart rate, reactions to fear and pain, and can quell an oncoming anxiety attack.

Breathing patterns can even alter our blood pH levels by manipulating the amount of trapped CO_2 in our blood using techniques like the Wim Hof method. This can increase our immunity to disease, decrease inflammation, or delay the release of lactic acid and decrease its negative effects on muscle tissue, which increases muscular endurance.

Finally, we learned that the nose knows. That the nose warms and filters the air of harmful toxins before it is delivered to the lungs. This aspect of nose breathing was critical for me because of my sensitivity to the cold, which often brough on bronchial spasm which then escalated into an asthma attack. We learned that the nose can be used to regulate depth and speed of respiration more fluently and releases nitric oxide, which then increases the amount of oxygen absorption with each breath.

It's all perfect. If you've followed along and practiced some of the techniques, then you should be feeling better and you're where you were designed to be: in complete sync with your biology and your environment, at least as far as your relationship with the element of air is concerned. That is a good start indeed and a critical step on your journey to badass. This is so important because otherwise there is no way to reach your maximum potential. Without correcting bad breathing habits and going from bad to baseline, you are making the road much more difficult than it has to be. This will hamper your progress as we move forward. You may go far but not as far as possible. In my life, because breathing was such a struggle, this fact was much more poignant and my diminished lung and cardio capacity more debilitating. But if you want the most from your mind (your brain uses oxygen too, better breathing also equals better thinking) and body, you must train your breath.

The purpose of embodied breathing is to be aware and grateful. Aware that the chemicals in the air and the biology and chemistry of our bodies are in harmony with each other. It blesses us as we bless it. The universe is on our side, it wants us to thrive. We were designed to work together. When we take air into our bodies, it fuels an alchemical fire that creates a passion for life. If we are aware of this, we are aware of our breathing, how we use that air, and most importantly, we don't take it for granted.

In an age of increasing instances of respiratory disease, COVID, flu, emphysema, asthma, we should be painfully aware of how important breathing is. From here on, we must continue to position breathing at the center of what we are trying to accomplish. This allows us to progress to more advanced methods of breath control that will increase capacity, efficiency, and endurance, which will have a transformative effect on the other systems of the body, taking us from where we are now to a higher level of physical and mental performance. We've gone from bad to baseline. From here we go from baseline to badass. But it starts with embodied breathing, taking it in, realizing and becoming conscious and aware of how the breath can affect you, and change you. That embodiment, that awareness, can now be used to further tune the dials of our biology to make us badass breathers.

Let's get to it.

Key Takeaways

- Don't take breath for granted.

- Be aware of how you breathe and how it effects your moods and your performance.

- Believe that how you breathe can be used to control your energy states, emotions, and even your body chemistry.

- Control your breath, control your life.

Core Techniques

Box breathing while being conscious of the breath. Pay attention to how the breath feels as you breathe it in. How it smells, its temperature. Feel how it expands your lungs as you fill them from your diaphragm. Hold. As you breathe out again feel the temperature of the air, the movement through your nose. Smile. Be grateful.

Advanced Techniques

Be aware of every breath. Control the pacing and the depth of the breaths you take, in and out. Become aware of how changing the pace and depth affects you, your energy state, your moods, your excitation and relaxation. Pacing is important. Normally, at rest, we should be breathing in about six inhalations a minute, if not less. Lengthen you exhale, slow your breathing. Calm your body and your mind. Become the best version of yourself. Visualize it. Open your eyes and become what you visualized.

Chapter 6 - Systema Breathing — Make Every Breath Count

W here do we go from here? We have gone from bad to baseline, but we have a little further to go to edge into badass territory. In the context of my journey, baseline meant that I had reached a level of breathing health where I reaped the benefits of the effort I expended to improve my cardiovascular endurance. I could keep up with others on the trail without feeling like I was constantly out of breath, I wasn't snoring, and, best of all, I rarely used my inhaler. I had gone from bad to base. Now I wanted to get to badass.

From here my journey took me down a few different paths, but it started with a Russian system of martial arts that places significant focus on breathing, called Systema. I later would realize that many martial arts consider breath control and the coordination of breathing and movement to be at their core, but I had never paid attention to that fact previously. After being introduced to Systema breathing practices, I discovered that elite athletes in martial arts and many other sports focused on breathwork. Breathing exercises are definitely at the forefront of Systema practices. In fact, most of what I found online about Systema related to breathing, and it was only as I dug deeper that I found it was a martial art.

Basic Systema exercises coordinate the breath with movement. More advanced exercises then focus on disrupting "normal" patterns of breathing and movement to ensure that the body can react quickly regardless of its position or the current breathing cycle. The two seem mutually exclusive; however, it became apparent that the coordination of breath with movement in a controlled fashion could be advantageous for power and stability, while training the body to react to any situation with "muscle memory" by purposely disrupting the connection between breathing and movement was also beneficial. In combat sports, where you must quickly fluctuate between attack and defense and are reacting to an opponent that is intentionally trying to surprise you, rapid responses are key. In these situations, you most likely will not have the luxury of consistently coordinating your breath with your movement. A fight is chaotic, so the body and breath need to adapt to defense and attack positions regardless of where you are in your breathing cycle.

The two basic tenants of Systema breathing, as defined by Vladimir Vasiliev in his book, *Let Every Breath ... – Secrets of the Russian Breath Masters*, are:

- Your breathing continues constantly, no matter what. (I believe there are exceptions to this, such as powerlifting, when core stability is required. In Systema, breath holds are used in training but not in everyday movement, in competition, or in combat.)

- Your breath permeates your entire body.

There are a lot of ways in which Systema techniques and practices manipulate breath within these two overarching principles. There are also breath holds, slow breathing, and body-weight exercises that combine or vacillate between slow/deep breathing and fast movements or fast/shallow breathing and slow movements. When I first started with Systema I used simple exercises that coordinated patterns of breathing with movement. What I found interesting was that these patterns could then be applied to any exercise or movement. I learned that there were patterns of breathing that seemed tailor-made for certain types of movement. Optimizing the breath optimized my performance of those activities. This enables Systema principles of breath to be incorporated into daily activities and workouts. The key difference was that when performing an exercise in Systema, the focus is on the breath and not on the movement itself. What you may find, as I did, is that your performance of the movement may improve. Reps may go up; weight or speed may increase. It was an interesting phenomenon that once again spoke to the importance of breath in all we do. Putting all this together into a badass breathing routine that combines exercises with training masks, weighted vests, and breath holds, will be covered in Chapter 8. What I will cover in this chapter are the principles that I learned from Systema and other similar systems and the core exercises and techniques I used to start inching my way above baseline into badass territory.

The exercises that follow integrate the core teachings of Systema breathing with what I had already learned about nose breathing and circumferential breathing to catapult me from baseline to badass. Although Systema exposed me to these concepts, there were other systems and exercises that use breath holds and breath control to increase performance. I'll be incorporating some of that knowledge into this chapter. However, it was Systema that first exposed me to the idea of performing breathwork with exercise and movement, which then evolved into incorporating breath holds and breathing disruption into my workouts as well.

Systema takes to a new level the control of positional breathing (breathing into certain areas of your body while in all types of positions, angles, and states of muscular contraction and relaxation), breathing patterns, and cadence. There are a few general suggestions I will make before we get to the individual exercises themselves that may help you get started.

I suggest using exercises with which you are familiar and already have a degree of muscle memory so that you can focus on the breath and not the movement. Start with simple body-weight exercises that have little risk of injury: air squats, pushups, pull-ups, planks, etc. I do not recommend using exercises that use weights, especially to start. Powerlifting exercises like the squat and deadlift use specific breathing patterns in order to strengthen and protect your core, as was covered in the chapter on circumferential breathing. That pattern should not be disrupted for these exercises as it could lead to injury. Combat sports and martial arts create a chaotic situation, where controlled breathing may not be possible and reaction to situations must be immediate. This is why Systema trains you to decouple breathing from motion so that you can react to chaos but at the same time shows that you can quickly regain control and power over your body and situation by controlling the breath.

The beginner exercises will match movement with breathing patterns. However, you will see that those patterns may be quite different than what you are normally used to. More advanced techniques will then decouple the breathing from the movement. When you first start, you may find this difficult. I know I did. It was here that I realized how my pattern of breathing had been married to certain movements. For example, taking in a breath while I lowered into a squat and releasing that breath on the way up was habitual. As you start disrupting this pattern, it may initially be frustrating. However, it should be a good frustration because you are learning at a neuromuscular level how your breath is tied to movement. In some cases, you may have to correct this because of poor breathing patterns, overbreathing, or a fast-breathing cadence. But even with correct breathing you will find some of these exercises to be challenging. I believe that is the point of these exercises: teaching you to be aware of the connection and allowing you to break it. Someone once told me that before you can break the rules of a system, you must learn what the rules are. In my opinion, Systema breathwork is great at accomplishing that, demonstrating through motion the rules of the respiratory system and then teaching you how to disrupt that and go to another level of control.

Systema as a martial art needs to ensure that reaction times are as fast as possible in response to changing combat conditions. If you are too slow to perform a block or a strike because you take that extra breath in or out in order to prepare, you'll lose the fight. The purpose of decoupling is to get your body used to reacting to the situation with highly trained muscle memory. I found this to be revelatory because I realized my reactions, breathing patterns, muscles, everything was tied together, and when I separated them I had some difficulties to start. Keep at it. Don't get frustrated. Concentrate on the breath and you will get there. What you will develop practicing these techniques will be well worth the frustration because they can be applied to many situations in daily life, such as when anxious, angry, or frustrated, and are not limited only to martial arts and combat situations.

Key Takeaways

- Systema is a martial art that places particular importance on breathwork. It uses a combination of coordinated movements with breath followed by more advanced exercises that decouple the breath from movement.

- The two overarching principles of Systema breathing are: Breathing is always continuous and every breath fills your whole body.

- Incorporating Systema breathwork into your routine will help you gain new levels of control of your breathing, regardless of the situations or positions you find yourself in.

- Systema breathwork is the next level of badassery.

Core Techniques

Important note: Always use the proper breathing techniques and apparatus that we have covered in previous chapters, unless otherwise noted. That means all exercises should be performed breathing completely through your nose using a circumferential breath with your diaphragm.

Tension Wave

This is one of the first Systema exercises I started with. Take a slow, relaxed breath in, and at the top of the breath begin to create a wave of tension from your toes upward to your head, contracting and tensing all muscles, joints and ligaments as you exhale. After a few repetitions, alter the flow by relaxing on the exhale and tensing on the inhale from head to toe. From here you can change the direction of the tensing, moving from head to toe, relax on inhale, tense on exhale, and then reverse again by tensing from head to toe on inhale while relaxing on exhale.

I often perform this exercise lying down in bed before getting up but found it also useful as a warmup before exercise. You can also perform it while standing as you become more comfortable with the process. Here is a detailed description of a tension wave:

Breathe in slowly, and as you do begin tensing every ligament, tendon, and muscle in your body from your toes, up through your feet, legs, hips, torso, chest, shoulders, neck, jaw, eyes, even your scalp. Try to do this in a wave of tension all the way to the top of your skull. Hold the breath and the tension for a few seconds. As you release the breath, begin to relax your body in the reverse wave starting with your head, jaw, neck, all the way back down to your toes. Do a few rounds in this direction and then reverse the direction by breathing in through your head and tensing in a similar wave pattern from your head down to your toes. Hold and then relax from your toes back up to your head.

Once you get comfortable with this pattern, you can then perform it with the opposite breathing pattern. Now you will tense when releasing the breath. Breathe in slow and relaxed; at the top of the breath, hold for a few moments and when you release begin to tense your body in a wave from your toes to your head. This will be the same wave pattern, only this time the tension occurs on the exhale and the relaxation on the inhale. Do this from toes to head for a few cycles and then repeat in the opposite direction, with the tension wave proceeding from head to toe on the out breath and relaxing on the inhale from toe to head.

As you get better at this, try to increase the speed of the wave and the cycles of breathing. Keep working at it, and then switch from one cycle to the next. Go from inhale tension wave from feet to head and then relaxing in the opposite direction from head to feet on the exhale. Then, on the next cycle, go immediately into tension wave from head to toe on inhale while relaxing on exhale from toe to head. Take a breath and then switch to tension wave on exhale and relaxion wave on inhale. Play around with different patterns.

That is the tension wave.

Body-Weight Exercises and Breathing Patterns

The following breathing exercises will combine simple movements with specific breathing patterns. Start with very simple body-weight exercises always focusing on the breathing pattern, not the movement itself. As I stated above, use movements where you already have some degree of muscle memory to allow you to focus on the breath and later incorporate more advance movements. If you are new to exercise I suggest performing the air squat and/or pushup. Do these exercises every day for a few sets. After a week or so, when you feel comfortable and the movement feels almost automatic, then you are ready. Armed with these core exercise movements you can then incorporate the below patterns of breathing.

For those of you who have been working out for a while, there may be a different set of challenges. As I mentioned previously, I discovered during this process that I had trained my body to work with breath patterns without realizing it. One such pattern was breathing out during exertion and breathing in during lowering or relaxing. Reversing this, modifying it, or even performing multiple breath cycles during a single action was very difficult at first. Don't get discouraged. For most this is not an easy task because along with the muscle memory of these movements there is an ingrained breathing pattern that we are now going to try and disrupt. The main movements I used were air squats, pushups, pullups, and variations of these (using wider stance, wall squats, jumps or ballistic movements, etc.). There is a surprising number of exercise variations that you can fool around with; when you add the variable of breath, the possibilities become almost infinite.

We will start with the breathing pattern I found most difficult, the halfway-change breath.

Halfway-Change Breath

In the halfway-change breath, you begin the exercise either inhaling or exhaling, and midway into the lowering or extension phase you switch to either an inhale or exhale. In Systema, all motion is led by the breath. Therefore, if you are going to start lowering your body from a plank position for a pushup, you will begin to inhale/exhale before you start the motion. Let's use pushups as an example of how to perform the halfway-change breath.

Get into a plank position with hands shoulder width apart on the floor. Begin to inhale, and then start to lower yourself towards the floor. As your body reaches the halfway point between full extension and the floor, begin to exhale until your chest touches the floor. Pause for a moment and begin your inhale, and then start to raise yourself from the floor, extending your arms. Halfway up, begin to exhale till you are at full extension (see Figure 7). This is one repetition.

Figure 7 – The Halfway Change Breath (Pushups)

You can also modify the pattern by beginning the motion with an exhale as you lower and switch to inhale halfway through the movement. Remember, this is a breathing exercise. You should strive to keep your body as relaxed as possible, which I found strangely easy as I began to focus more on the breath than the movement. I do not count reps; my attention is on the breathing pattern. As we move into other exercises, this concept will become more and more important; the focus should always remain on the breath. It might surprise you to find that your performance of these exercises improves. My rep count went up in each exercise without me realizing it until one day I did count the number of reps and found that I had surpassed my previous personal bests.

The Stretch-Your-Breath Exercise

The stretch-your-breath exercise utilizes the Systema principle of symmetric breathing, ensuring that inhales, exhales, and holds follow a symmetrical pattern. Think box breathing. Stretch your breath is one example of a symmetrical pattern. However, I have found that symmetrical patterns benefit other exercises by balancing breathing and movement and ensuring that you are properly training both inhalation and exhalation muscles. Blood oxygen and CO_2 balance is also maintained via the breath holds within the exercises to ensure a buildup and tolerance to CO_2.

Again, you can use any movement you feel comfortable with. Stretch your breath uses a symmetrical pyramid count for each repetition. This means that the number of breaths, repetitions, etc. start from a number, go up, and then work their way back to the number you started with. In this example I'll use the pushup and a pyramid count that governs the length of the inhale and exhale cycle in conjunction with the speed of each repetition.

To perform stretch your breath, begin your inhale and lower your body to the floor with a count of one. Maintain the same counting pace and rhythm throughout the exercise. This is another time when a metronome can come in handy to maintain a regular pace count throughout the exercise. Pause. Begin your exhale and push up to extension to a count of one. On the next repetition, begin your inhale; but this time, extend your breath lowering yourself to a count of two, pause, begin your exhale and raise yourself to a count of two. On subsequent repetitions extend the inhale/exhale by one count (e.g., three count, four count, five count, etc.) Whatever count you go to, make sure you are relaxed and can pyramid back to the starting number. Once you reach a comfortable count, let's say four, then reverse the process, keeping the same count cadence, back down the pyramid till you reach the base: one, two, three, four; then one, two, three; then one, two; then one. That is a set. As with all exercises, you can modify this to begin the downward phase of the pushup with an exhale and the pushup phase with an inhale. My suggestion, and what I do, is begin every set with a different pattern. If on set one I started with an inhale, then on set two I begin with an exhale. That is stretch your breath.

Slow Motion and Burst Breathing

In the slow motion exercise you will perform a movement very slowly to a specific count. For this you can use either a timer or a metronome to assist the count. During the execution of the exercise, breathe slow and deep. As an example, I'll use the squat performed with a 20 count to reach the lower position and a 20 count to rise.

Get into a squat-ready position with your feel slightly wider than shoulder width apart, and begin to lower yourself slowly as you begin your count. Do not jerk downward but maintain a constant, easy motion throughout the entirety of the repetition. Lower yourself slowly and smoothly while counting to 20. At the count of 20, your thighs should be parallel to the floor. Now slowly and smoothly begin to rise, starting your count from one to 20 (see Figure 8).

Starting Position   10 Count Position   20 Count Position

Figure 8 – Slow Motion with the Squat

This exercise helps to train your body awareness and pacing. It is also useful in disrupting the normal inhale, exhale paradigm when performing a repetition, as most people are used to doing one complete breath cycle (inhale/pause/exhale) for every repetition performed.

Now we can add burst breathing. As you lengthen the count for performing a slow repetition, the exercise will become more strenuous. This is where burst breathing comes in. This is taking short and sharp inhales and exhales through your nose. As your muscles start to fatigue and you feel the burn of lactic acid, begin to burst breathe. Do this as quickly as needed to overcome the pain and fatigue but remember to keep the same pace of the movement and count.

This addition to the slow-motion movement further enhances your ability to engage different breathing patterns during a single exercise or repetition.

Bundled-Breathing Patterns

In bundled breathing, you perform multiple repetitions of an exercise during a phase of the breathing cycle (inhale, hold, and exhale). I also like to use pyramid schemes with bundled breathing. For this exercise I will use the squat as an example.

The simplest form of this pattern is to perform two repetitions with a single breath cycle. For example, take in a breath as you begin to descend into the squat and continue to breathe in slowly as you reach parallel and return to a standing position. Now begin your exhale and descend into the squat, slowing your exhale as you reach parallel and then continuing to exhale till you are standing up straight again. That is one bundled-breath cycle but encompasses two squat repetitions.

From here you can increase the number of repetitions you perform for each phase of the breath. Next in the cycle would be two repetitions of the squat on the inhale, and two on the exhale. Then three, then four on subsequent cycles. Remember to leave enough energy to pyramid back down.

Once comfortable with these patterns, you can also incorporate breath holds as part of the cycle. When I incorporate breath holds, I always use them on the exhale with empty lungs to increase CO_2 tolerance. You can start by keeping them symmetrical. For example, doing two repetitions on inhale, two repetitions on the exhale and then hold for two repetitions. If the holds become a limiting factor in performing repetitions of symmetrical sets, then you can vary how may repetitions of the movement you do with the hold. In some cases, you may do four squats on an exhale but can only perform one squat on the hold and then do four squats on the inhale. You can fool around with the count. But the hold does not have to be symmetrical with the inhale/exhale if it is extremely uncomfortable and therefore limiting the number of repetitions you can do during the other breath phases. However, try to maintain the symmetry for the inhale and exhale phases as this is the main point of the exercise.

The Quick Freeze and Segmented Tension

I wrote about the tension-wave exercise earlier where you breathe in through your feet or the top of your head, tensing every body part as you breathe in and then relaxing in the reverse direction as you exhale. Another version of this is the quick freeze, in which you tense every muscle in your body simultaneously as you inhale and then simultaneously release and relax on the exhale. Then reverse the pattern and tense on exhale and relax on inhale. When I say every muscle, I mean everything: your lips, jaw, eyelids, you name it. Try to make your hair tense. Same with the relaxation: feel tension ebbing away from every part of your body. This exercise and the ones that follow enhance your awareness of your whole body – the muscles, tendons, and ligaments – that then allows you to control and relax them.

As you advance from tension wave to quick freeze, you can move on to segmented tension exercises. This is where the principles of tension and relaxation are the same, but now you focus on creating tension and/or relaxation in a specific part of your body. You inhale through specific areas or zones of your body while creating the tension. As an example, you could tense both legs, both arms, back, stomach, chest or neck on the inhale, and then relax them on the exhale. Practice this with multiple parts of your body or a combination of parts, say your right hand and your left foot. In each case you will breathe into these parts of the body, tense, pause/hold, exhale and relax completely, then reverse the pattern like with the tension wave where you will exhale and tense, inhale and relax.

The more advanced form of segmented tension is to relax a specific area of your body while tensing everything else. For instance, relax your arms or stomach while tensing every other part of your body. This is a difficult exercise and progress may come slowly. In this example, if you find that you are tensing your arms or stomach (those parts that should be relaxed) as you tense the rest of your body then you still need more practice. You can also try to start small and pick something like your hand, foot, or even a finger or toe to stay relaxed as you tense everything else.

As of this writing I still find this difficult. I do not achieve it with every practice. But I have found that even attempting it creates a more complete body awareness. It also builds a deeper understanding of how breath plays a role in the relaxation and tension of the body and muscles. I have found that if I breathe into the area I want to relax and focus on that area, while simultaneously tensing the rest of my body, I can achieve the desired result. This also takes a lot of visualization, which creates a closer bond between breathing and your mental state and creativity. This exercise and the rest that follow not only make a stronger connection between breath and body but also between breath and mind, and the ever elusive "spirit" or energy. It was while performing this exercise that I came to believe I could tap into such powerful resources.

Body-Segment Breathing

Breathing through body segments is similar to the quick-freeze and tension-wave exercises, but in this case the entire exercise is performed while completely relaxed. In segment breathing, you inhale through one part of your body and then exhale through another. For example, inhale through your arms and exhale out through your legs. Inhale through your right arm and then breathe out the left. Inhale through your head and out your tailbone. In through your chest, out through your back. You can do this with any body part; the more practiced you become, the more focused the exercise becomes. In through the right kidney, out through the left. In one finger, out another.

Visualization is another important tool for this exercise. Imagine you are filling every cell within that part of the body as you inhale, and then push the air out another part while releasing all tension in that organ, muscle, or tendon that you are exhaling through. This is a powerful technique with which I have had much success. I've released neck and back pain, muscle soreness, and alleviated the pain of injuries while performing this exercise. For this purpose, I inhale through an opposing muscle, for instance inhale through my throat and exhale out the back of the neck in the region where I have pain or tension, slowly releasing all that pain and tension. This can also be accomplished at times by breathing in and out through the same pain infected area; however, I have found that this opposing breathing pattern works better for me. You can experiment with different body parts and patterns. This experimentation will help you gain deeper insights into the various areas in which you hold tension, as well as give you the ability to control that which you didn't know you could. You cannot control that which you don't know exists. Therefore, becoming aware of your body and its capabilities is the first step towards being able to control it. These segment-tension exercises demonstrate this principle very well.

Feel the Pulse

Feel the pulse is yet another extension of body awareness and the one I have the most difficulty with. This is a great way to end a breathing session or a workout.

The first goal is to simply become aware of your pulse and be able to feel it in different areas of your body. You can do this initially by searching for your pulse on your wrist or neck, but the goal is to become aware of it without needing to do that. Once you find a place where it is easier for you to become aware of the pulse, focus on it. If it's in the temples, chest, or ears, focus on that and hear the pulse. Let that expand so that you can feel the pulse within your whole body. Focus. Feel. Now, breathe in coordination with the pulse. For every three beats do one inhale, three beats on exhale. As you get better you can include holds: three beats inhale, three beats hold, three beats exhale, three beats hold, again. Just like box breathing. The goal, once you've created this synchronization, is to slow the breath down and as a result, begin to slow your pulse. This is why I like doing this at the end of a workout, because it is easier to detect my pulse when my heart is beating harder than at rest, and it's a great way to cool down. With each round, slow the breath and slow the heartbeat. Slower. Slower. You will feel relaxed. Your pulse will slow and become more consistent, but strangely you will feel it more as it pulses through your entire being in time with the breath.

For precision athletes like archers or shooters, this is an important skill as it is best to release the shot at the natural pause of breath and beat; but to be able to control this, we must become aware of it. Regardless of your goals, being able to control your heart rate and blood pressure by performing this exercise will give you yet another level of body breath awareness that will pay dividends in your performance regardless of whether or not you are an archer, a martial artist, weight lifter, business person, or artist. Great breathing equals great performance. Once you match the pattern, cadence, and amount of breathing with the demands of the task you will optimize everything you do.

Advanced Techniques

The All-Together Exercise

Once a week or so I like to include many of these patterns and breath holds into a dynamic routine that trains the body and mind to adapt to the chaos and demands of real life. This is an advanced exercise and should be attempted only after mastering each of the included exercises and patterns separately. What is below is just an example. As I said, the goal should be to make this dynamic, random, and chaotic. Try to come up with new and creative ways to make this exercise more dynamic. Bottom line, what follow is just an example and every session should be different.

Start with the tension-wave breathing pattern while standing. Perform a few rounds of this pattern while rotating the direction of the wave and the breathing pattern to ensure symmetry. Breathe in through the head and down the body while tensing, breathe out relaxing in the opposite direction. After a few rounds, inhale from toes to head tensing and then relaxing in the opposite direction. Now tense while exhaling, pushing the air from your head to toes and then relax in the opposite direction as you inhale. After a few rounds, use this same pattern but reverse the flow so you are tensing while exhaling the air from toes to head then relaxing in the opposite direction while inhaling.

That was the warm up. From here you will not follow a specific sequence. The idea is to perform various activities using a different breathing pattern for each movement and include random breath holds in the process. Once you start moving, don't stop until the cool down. In between movements you can walk, roll, or jog.

When I perform this, the movement phase only lasts between five to 10 minutes, and the whole session from beginning to end rarely goes more than 15-20 minutes unless I feel so relaxed at the end that I just decide to sit and relax for longer, which happens frequently.

Here is an example of the movement phase:

Use the halfway-change breath pattern while doing pushups. Don't worry about the number of repetitions on any of the exercises; this is breathwork. At a certain random point of the exercise, perform a hold. It is difficult to make this truly random unless you have a friend doing it with you who can all of a sudden call out, "Hold!" When by myself, anytime the word "hold" pops into my head I perform one. Whatever movement I'm doing I continue at the same pace and rhythm, regardless of where I am in the breathing cycle. From here I may do some forward rolls or walk while performing various breathing patterns. I may walk 10 paces on an out breath, hold 10 paces, 10 paces on an inhale, roll, with deep, slow breathing. Hold. Perform super slow squats with burst breathing for a count of 20 down, then 20 up. Jog holding my breath for 20 paces, walk inhaling for 10, exhale for 10.

Now I may move to performing an extended breath with pullups using a pyramid scheme, increasing the length of inhale and exhale for each cycle up and then down the pyramid. One, two, three, four, five; then five, four, three, two, one. I may also add holds during this pyramid. The hold should be random. Don't worry about what phase you are in. If the word "hold" pops into your head or you are listening to a song and designate a certain repeated phrase as a command to perform a breath hold, then you are on the right track. If you are in the middle of an inhale or exhale and the word pops up – hold. Hold until it either becomes uncomfortable and you experience air hunger or keep this random as well by releasing the hold on the same word or a different lyric in the song. You get the idea.

Roll with slow breathing. Perform a bundled-breathing pyramid with squats. One repetition on an inhale, one on the exhale. Two repetitions on inhale, two repetitions on exhale, etc. Then, once you reach a certain number, four for example, pyramid back down till you end again on one inhale for one repetition and one exhale for one repetition. Hold. Perform some pullups while holding on exhale. Once it become uncomfortable, breathe in slowly and fully. Walk. Breathe slowly. Take in flickers of air through your nose that are so small that you can barely feel or hear it, filling only your nostrils. Walk. Now lay down and feel your pulse. Synchronize your breath with the pulse. Three beats, breath in; three beats, breath out. Slow your breath. Feel your pulse slowing. Slower. Slower. Relax. Feel. Enjoy.

What I enjoy about this is it adds randomness and creativity. You can tweak the sequence and intentionally disrupt yourself to improve your adaptability, and it puts many of the patterns into practice. You can do multiple exercises without changing the pattern. Do halfway-change breaths and move from pushups to squats without changing the pattern, even during the transition. Use the pattern while getting to a standing position. This will truly make you aware of your breath as you simultaneously coordinate it and decouple it from your movements. Enjoy.

At the end of the day, you want to become capable of controlling your breath and understanding how to use it in any situation. There is a pattern that will optimize performance and prepare your body to respond appropriately to any situation, whether that means it's time to fight, relax, defend, give an important presentation, relieve depression, soothe anxiety, or heal your body. This is why Systema was so important in my journey because it made breath training practical. It trains you to breathe based on the situational needs and builds the awareness that enables you to know when to trigger a certain pattern.

Armed with that knowledge we can now strengthen our breathing muscles and build up our resistance to CO_2 and lactic acid. Then we combine everything we have learned, add some tools and technology, and become true badass breathers.

CHAPTER 7 - BREATH PACING, BREATH HOLDS, AND CO2 TOLERANCE

As I have mentioned previously, overbreathing is an issue. This chapter will go into more depth as to why that is and how to correct it. Overbreathing is a disruption of what should be a natural breathing pattern caused by many of the issues we've covered in other parts of this book, such as increased CO_2 sensitivity, upper chest breathing, mouth breathing, and stress. Aside from the corrections we have already implemented during the course of the book, such as switching to nose breathing and circumferential breathing, what else needs to be considered to prevent overbreathing? Pacing. Pacing is measured by how many breaths we take in a minute and the volume of air and oxygen we exchange as a result. To prevent overbreathing we need to slow that pace, decreasing the volume of air while increasing the amount of oxygen absorbed with each breath through a proper balance of blood CO_2 and oxygen concentrations. In short, we need to breathe the way we were designed to.

So, why is overbreathing a problem? Number one, it reduces the efficiency of our red blood cells in absorbing the oxygen we breathe and making it available to the body. When we overbreathe we pull in too much air, resulting in CO_2 levels staying flat. When CO_2 levels don't rise, the trigger to release hemoglobin-bound oxygen molecules is never pulled. This results in us breathing more but not absorbing what we are taking in. Average pacing for most adults is between 12 and 20 breaths a minute, with an average intake of half a liter per breath. Optimal pacing and volume should be roughly half this amount per minute. Just as we have become a society of overeaters that are starving ourselves obese by constantly eating food that does not have the nutrition our bodies need to thrive, we are also depriving our bodies of the oxygen we require by taking in too much air and overtaxing our breathing apparatus in the process.

The second reason overbreathing is a problem is that it hinders our performance. If CO_2 levels in our blood never rise, our sensitivity to CO_2 increases, which causes us to always feel starved of oxygen because any slight rise in CO_2 levels will flip the panic switch that tells our bodies we need more oxygen. This again results in a cycle where increasing sensitivity causes more feelings of air hunger, which we attempt to remedy by increasing both pace and volume. Again, a self-perpetuating shit cycle.

Then, think of what all this overbreathing is doing to our lungs, diaphragm, and ancillary breathing muscles. You are expending a lot of energy to supply oxygen to your body, and when carrying out athletic activity your body will prioritize air exchange over muscle performance. We are burdening our entire breathing anatomy by overbreathing, and none of that extra air is being absorbed. It's like strapping on a 50-pound weight vest while trying to do ballet. But what if you could breathe half as much yet absorb more oxygen and reduce your sensitivity to CO_2 levels so that the body takes longer to feel starved of oxygen? That is where pacing comes in.

Suffice it to say that all the corrections we have discusses thus far work synergistically to help correct our breathing. If you incorporate nose breathing, circumferential breathing with the diaphragm, and now pacing they will all compound the results you will see and feel. Therefore, I encourage you to look at these corrections in tandem because I believe you will see faster results.

So, what is the correct pacing? Less. When saying that, it is not just about pacing but the amount of air we inhale with each breath. It is slower, yes, but it is also less. Fewer inhales and exhales with a smaller volume. How much less? That can be complicated but most experts agree it should be somewhere between six to 10 breaths per minute. At the end of the day, what matters is that you are breathing optimally for the metabolic and energy needs of the body, and that is obviously influenced by many factors. However, if we train to desensitize our bodies to CO_2 and become more aware of how we breathe and how correct breathing feels, we will be able to adjust our pace to match the needs of the body for any given situation. So first we need to build up our CO_2 resistance, and for that there are pacing, volume-decreasing, and breath-holding exercises. We will start with pacing and decreasing volume and then move on to breath holds.

Training to decrease your pace is simple. Breathe in lightly through your nose in such a way that you can't hear your breath, or if you put your finger just below your nose you cannot feel the intake of breath with your finger. Inhale for three seconds and then exhale slowly, trying to do so in a way that you don't hear or feel it for a count of four. After a few repetitions, try to lengthen the exhale to five seconds, then six, etc. with the same three-second inhale. Longer exhales produce higher carbon dioxide levels, creating a higher aerobic endurance and increasing VO2 max (a measure of the maximum amount of oxygen your body can utilize during exercise), which is one of the best gauges of cardiorespiratory fitness.

The aim of this exercise is to continue to lengthen the inhale to decrease our bodies' sensitivity to rising CO2 levels so that during normal breathing we do not feel starved of air and can breathe at a slower rate with lower volume, without experiencing air hunger. As always, monitoring is key. You need to check in with your body periodically to gauge how you are breathing and the pacing, and consciously slow it down.

By decreasing your sensitivity to CO2 and giving your breathing muscles a much-needed chance to recoup, you can now advance to the next level of decreasing CO2 sensitivity with breath holds.

Breath Holds

The second method for increasing resistance to CO2 and increasing VO2 max is hypoxic, hypoventilation training, more commonly known as breath holds. The breath holds I cover here work differently than those in the Wim Hof method. I mentioned in that chapter that the Wim Hof method should be paired with a breath-hold exercise that builds tolerance to rising levels of CO2. The Wim Hof method works in such a way that CO2 levels take a longer time to rise towards baseline, which allows you to hold your breath for longer, increasing oxygen levels and creating an alkaline state in the body. The breath-hold exercises we use here will increase tolerance to rising CO2 levels. Decreasing sensitivity to CO2 results in increased performance, increased lactic acid tolerance, increased resistance to pain, and reduced anxiety and stress. All of which is part and parcel of becoming a badass breather. I perform all my breath holds with empty lungs. Therefore, I exhale fully before I begin the exercise, whether that is pushups, pullups, sprinting, etc. That includes when I use a training mask, which I will cover in the next chapter. There are so many different variations and patterns but I'll give you my favorites, the ones I use daily and weekly.

Key Takeaways

- Our modern breathing patterns have increased our sensitivity to CO_2, which has resulted in overbreathing.

- Overbreathing creates a feedback loop in which CO_2 levels never rise to the point where hemoglobin-trapped O_2 is released into the blood, resulting in feelings of air hunger which cause increased breathing pace and volume.

- Overbreathing taxes our lungs and diaphragm, resulting in more energy being utilized to prioritize oxygen intake instead of muscle performance.

- Slowing pace and lowering volume increase the body's CO_2 tolerance, allowing for the release of O_2 from hemoglobin. Increased oxygen absorption with each breath equates to less energy being used for air exchange so more is available for enhanced mental and athletic performance.

Core Techniques

Slower and Less – The Silent, Slow Breath

Start with a slow, silent breath through the nose for three seconds. Put your finger below your nose and try to pull in the air so slowly that you can't feel the air going in or out. After the inhale, let out the air slowly for a count of four. The goal here is to keep the inhale slow and silent for three seconds and to do a slow and silent exhale, extending the time taken for the exhale by one second each cycle. For example: First breath is a three seconds inhale, followed by a four second exhale; next is a three second inhale, and a five second exhale, etc. When you reach an exhale count that begins to feel uncomfortable, try to maintain that pattern for a few cycles. For example, if you start to feel air hunger when you reach three-second inhales with a seven-second exhale, try to maintain that pattern until it become very uncomfortable or pyramid back down, decreasing your exhale by one second until you get back to three second inhale, four second exhale.

I love using a training mask (more on these in the next chapter) with this exercise, because it amplifies breathing noise and you have to breathe very slowly in order to not hear your breath. I will often use this method when sitting at my desk while working, slowing the breath and volume till my breathing is no longer audible. The mask allows you to perform this exercise hands-free, allowing you to get work done while getting in some additional breathwork. The more resistance you use on the mask the more difficult it is to maintain a silent breath. In addition, the mask pools CO_2 so you are pulling in more with each breath, which will also increase the exercise's efficiency in training your body to become less sensitive to CO_2.

Breath-Hold Diaphragm Activation

I do breath-hold diaphragm activation as a warmup before other breathwork exercises. It creates diaphragm awareness. Remember, these are gentle breaths.

Take a soft, silent breath in through your nose and then out through your nose. When your lungs are empty, pinch your nose with your fingers to hold your breath for 10-15 seconds. While pinching, try to gently breathe in and out of your nose.

Feel your abdomen moving in and out while you try to breathe.

Let go of your nose and resume normal breathing for one minute, and then repeat three to five times.

Increasing Breath Holds During Activity

I use the below technique almost daily at the end of most of my workouts. The example below is walking but I have also substituted other exercises and movements with this breathing pattern, such as with pushups, pullups, and air squats. Again, all the exercises I perform during breath holds use bodyweight only. I do not perform any breath holds under load. I've also used this pattern when wearing a training mask, which increases the stress on the diaphragm and builds your breathing muscles when you are breathing in between the holds.

Take a normal breath in and out of your nose while walking slowly or performing a no-load exercise (I suggest you start with walking till you get used to the pattern, as this allows for better focus on the breathing itself). After a minute or so, breathe out and pinch your nose with your fingers to hold the breath, or simply hold your breath (if wearing a mask or the movement does not allow you to pinch your nose).

Continue walking with the breath held till you reach moderate air hunger. I usually do this for 10-20 steps, increasing by five to 10 steps for each successive round. For example, on round one I walk 10 paces with breath held creating a moderate air hunger. Round two I walk 15 paces, and round three, 20 paces.

When you feel moderate to strong air hunger, release and breathe in slowly for a few paces and then stop. Control your inhales so they are not fast and deep. Do not gulp air. Use your diaphragm and nose to control the inhale and keep it slow.

When you stop, take six short, slow flickers of breath in through your nose that just barely fill your nostrils.

Begin walking again, taking in 10 normal breaths through the nose.

Then begin another round of the breath-hold pattern.

After the second or third cycle, I will then begin to jog during the breath hold till the air hunger is strong and I begin to feel muscle contractions in my diaphragm and throat. I will do two to three more cycles of this while jogging, but I will increase the number of paces or distance that I jog with each cycle with the air hunger becoming more uncomfortable.

In between cycles, use the same pattern with normal breathing for a few paces: six short flickers of air through the nose, then 10 normal breaths and then repeat the breath hold cycle.

All in all, I perform about six to eight breath holds during the whole exercise, after which I will slow to a walk and breathe normally for two to three minutes. You do not have to jog or perform other exercises for this to be effective. I've used it pacing in my living room or at times even just while reading. I'll try to increase the number of paragraphs I can read during the hold. However, my favorite is to finish a workout with this routine using the walking and jogging combination.

Advanced Techniques

Hypoxic Training

I have found that if I can make things simple and add them easily to my normal routine I'm much more likely to keep up with them. Therefore, I tend to add short breathwork sessions to my existing routines, which ensures that I'm getting the benefit of focusing on breathwork but without the hassle of having to devote a large chunk of time to it. Hypoxic training is something that you can easily add to almost any routine and is effective in decreasing CO_2 sensitivity. I use this most often while working out, and it can be used anytime unless you are trying to reach a personal best. Again, to defend against injury I only suggest breath holds with non-load bearing exercises where core strength is not needed. For these reasons I typically use pushups, ballistic pushups, air squats, box jumps, pullups, etc.

The pattern is simple. Start by breathing out, hold your breath, and then begin the movement. Continue performing the exercise until you feel a moderate to strong desire to breathe. When you breathe try to do it slowly but continue the movement. Use long, slow, deep breaths. As you advance you can then do another round within the same set. For instance, you hold your breath for five pushups, breathe slow and deep for five pushups and then hold again, following this pattern till you are done with the set.

Another variation is to perform a certain number of repetitions during each set with your breath held but during a different phase of the exercise, such as the beginning, middle, or final repetitions of the set. I like to vary it up per workout. I will then increase the number of reps that I complete with a held breath during each successive set. For example, I would hold my breath for five pushups during set one, 10 for set two, 15 for set three, etc. On day one I may perform all the breath holds at the start of the exercise and then breathe normally during the rest of the set, while on day two I'd perform the breath hold on the last five, 10, 15, etc. reps of the set. You can also add a pyramid scheme here by holding the breath for a five, 10, 15 repetition pattern and then pyramid back down from 15 by doing 10 and then five repetitions per breath hold.

Another breath-hold variation I like to use is what I call the one for one. This is the ratio between the number of reps done with a breath hold and the number of recovery breaths I get between sets. For example, let's say I'm doing pullups. I start out by exhaling to empty lungs and then do a set of five repetitions. I now take five fully-controlled, slow nose breaths to recover. On the fifth breath I exhale to empty lungs and do another set of five. I continue this pattern until I can no longer manage five reps while performing a hold or I begin to pyramid down. For instance, if after doing four sets I find that I can only manage four reps of pullups, then I only get four recovery breaths. I'll do this till I can only manage three reps, in which case I only get three recovery breaths. You get the idea. The ratio always stays the same. However many reps you get during the hold equals the number of recovery breaths you get in between sets. You'll be amazed at how this can act as a motivator for doing extra reps.

Remember that during these breath-holding exercise we are not focused on the number of reps but in increasing our CO_2 tolerance and creating Homeric stress in order to help our body adapt to low oxygen conditions and train the breathing muscles. To this aim it is always good to add variations and play around with different exercises. Breathing adaptability and flexibility is our goal, so challenging yourself with different variations is key.

In this next chapter I will take this to a whole new badass level by including training masks and plate carriers.

Chapter 8 - Badass Breathing Warrior — Masks, Plate Carriers, and Straws, Oh My!

In this chapter I will go through the tools I use to strengthen my breathing muscles and how I use them to help me regulate the volume and intensity of my workouts during various phases of training. Then I will cover the core principles used to help you build your own customized badass breathing routine to meet your needs and goals, while providing examples of the exercises and routines that I use. Many of the exercises you will find here should seem familiar at this point. There are some new ones but most are an extension of exercises and breath holds that have been reviewed throughout this book.

Training masks and plate carriers add another dimension to your breathwork, increasing the stress on the breathing muscles by making it more difficult to breathe while performing the exercises. The mask, in particular, will increase breathing resistance and tolerance to rising CO_2 levels because CO_2 will pool in the mask. The mask will also make it difficult to take full breaths during the recovery phase, making you experience air hunger throughout a workout which will further increase your tolerance to CO_2. But before we get to masks and plate carriers, let's talk straws.

Straws

Straws? you ask. This may seem an odd training device. It is also the only training tool I use that forces me to use my mouth. There are snorkel-like devices designed to help you regulate the breath or make it harder to breathe through a long tube with increasing levels of resistance, but for me, I've found straws to be cheap and just as effective.

The straw exercise is simple but not easy. Pinch your nose and breathe through the straw for a number of repetitions, inhaling all the way in and all the way out using your diaphragm and extending the exhale until you feel you have completely emptied your lungs. Sounds easy, right? Do this for five to 10 reps and you may think differently. Breathing through a straw increases the strength of your diaphragm and your ancillary exhale muscles. Focus a lot of attention on the exhale, ensuring that you are breathing out slowly and that you fully empty your lungs by pulling in your diaphragm and hollowing out your midsection.

One of the benefits of using the straw is that it forces a slower exhale because there is only so much air you can force down the straw at a time. This will help extend your exhale, which has the added benefit of slowing your breathing pace. I use bendy straws because I can increase the resistance by bending the straw in a loop and now use two straws taped together with multiple bends to increase resistance. This one will really make you feel your diaphragm like nothing else I have used and, as I said, it is a simple and cheap tool to use. Thus far, it's my most inexpensive piece of workout gear.

Training Masks

Finding the Right Training Mask

There are a number of different training masks out there that simulate high-altitude training and increase breathing resistance. Training with a mask is formally called inspiratory flow resistant loading (IFRL) because it adds resistance to the act of breathing, making it more difficult to pull in air. Experts in pulmonary performance believe that IFRL with a training mask can improve respiratory muscle strength by 20-50%! Sounds like a good tool for those looking to become badass. Designed to make it more difficult to breathe, training masks make you work harder to supply your body with baseline levels of oxygen and are therefore simulating what it would be like to train at higher altitudes. By doing this, training masks will also increase tolerance to rising CO_2 levels, increase the strength and endurance of the breathing muscles (the diaphragm and supporting musculature), and get you mentally used to the fear associated with having your breathing restricted. There are any number of sports or situations in which breathing could become restricted or interrupted: diving, spear fishing, jujitsu, grappling, etc. and for those not used to this feeling it can create immediate panic. Getting comfortable with longer periods of air hunger, or even intermittent periods of not being able to breathe at all, are important preparations for these activities. However, even if you are not into spear fishing or grappling this training will increase your body's ability to deal with periods when you cannot get enough oxygen and increase your ability to absorb oxygen and use it efficiently.

More importantly, you will train your mind to deal with this panic and fear, which then adds another level to your mental game and your ability to deal with all types of stress and anxiety.

The breathing resistance created by these training masks can be modified to go from barely noticeable to severe and when combined with exercise can be indispensable in making you a better breather and increasing your performance. For a list of training masks that I have used please visit . There are many training mask variations. The important feature of a training mask is that it has a dial or lever that can be used to increase and decrease the breathing resistance. Some training masks have valves systems with varying degrees of resistance. In order to modify the resistance, you must swap out the valves and/or their configuration. This is not optimal for performing the exercises the way I have outlined them. However, if you want to use a valve-based mask, the other option is to select a valve configuration that makes it noticeably difficult for you to breathe while resting and at those times in the exercise where I suggest increasing the resistance, use a breath hold. The one caveat to this approach is that when using the mask my goal is usually to breathe during the performance of the entire exercise in order to strengthen my breathing muscles. I will, at times, use a mask to add difficulty to the breath-hold exercises outlined in the previous chapter, but the exercises in this chapter differ because I'm usually breathing throughout and using the mask to create oxygen deprivation, not breath holds. This puts a constant strain on the breathing muscles and increases their strength and endurance. The other benefit of this is that you can use the mask during almost any activity where it doesn't compromise safety, such as running, weight lifting, yoga, kettle bells, etc. During these exercises the mask is an indispensable tool because it allows you to use the proper breathing patterns that support your core. The mask will make you work harder for that core-supporting breath, but as long as you can inflate your diaphragm as needed to support your core you can use the mask to add breathing resistance. Never compromise on safety. If you find that you are unable to take in the breath needed to support your core, lower the mask's resistance, or remove it.

Use of the mask can also turn almost any activity into a breathwork session. For instance, I will often wear one while mowing the lawn. This is not usually a physically-taxing exercise, but with the addition of the mask it becomes 90 minutes of straining breathwork. This may not sound like much, but once you start using the mask you will notice the significant effect your breathing and the amount of oxygen you can pull into your body has on your ability to perform. I have yet to complete mowing my lawn with the mask configured in a way where it provides the most breathing resistance. At some point I will have to lower the resistance a few degrees in order to continue. Using the mask in this way, even if you use it at the minimum setting, will also get you mentally used to having your breath restricted, which is surprisingly stressful; therefore, it is good to get used to this while having your mind occupied on another task where the focus isn't necessarily on the breath. Performing an ordinary physical task while wearing a mask is another great way to incorporate breathwork into your daily and weekly routine without having to set aside time just for breathwork.

Another great use of the mask is to increase workout intensity. As I get closer to competitions, say a week or 10 days before, I start using a mask during my normal training to prepare. This helps to decrease volume and increase intensity without adding additional weight or resistance the way you would normally. The reason? I can get a great cardio workout in a shorter period of time or by using less repetitions. This allows my muscles to recover while also keeping the intensity and cardio up. For instance, leading up to a Spartan race I may do

130 burpees every morning. But as the competition draws nearer, I may start to decrease the volume to 90, 60, and on the week of the event maybe only 30. Once I start to decrease volume I add the mask. This ensures that the resistance is there and that I continue to train my breathing muscles and cardio without having to spend hours running or doing burpees, which would have a negative effect on my performance in the race by not allowing me to fully recover.

Masks can also be used to ramp up the intensity towards the end of a high-volume, high-intensity cycle. As I'll explain in future books, I use a periodization scheme for my workouts. A high-volume, high-intensity cycle is designed to increase the body's adaptability to rising workloads and stress. There are only so many hours in the day, and one of the methods I use to increase this stress is to include the mask and plate carrier in my workouts, especially towards the end of this cycle.

As you can see, masks are a versatile training tool and, in my opinion, every badass breather should utilize one.

Plate Carriers

It's important for badass breath training that a plate-carrier system has the capability to add weights in both the front and back and that the area covering your midsection (your diaphragm) can be tightened with some type of Velcro or elastic belt system. My favorite is the 5.11+ TacTec® Plate Carrier and it is the only one I use. However, there are other carriers available that will fit these specifications. Focus should be on finding a carrier that secures plates over the diaphragm (front and back) and has a belly strap that is tightened to hold the plates against your body, sandwiching your midsection, which creates the resistance we are aiming for. For most exercises I have 11.2-pound plates in front and back and cinch the belt tight enough that at rest it puts pressure on my diaphragm when I take in a normal breath. I also have 20-pound plates but I only use those for running and hiking and not for specific breathwork training sessions. I suggest that you choose what is right for you, including potentially starting without weights and relying on the pressure created by the belt system alone to create diaphragm breathing resistance as you perform various exercises.

The plate carrier, like the training mask, is another tool to increase breathing resistance. I don't have specific exercises (except for one which I'll cover) that I use it for. I use it to increase the pressure on my diaphragm, making it more difficult to take in a breath. For the most part I can or will use it with any of the exercises in this book to add another level of difficulty. Combined with the mask, this is a powerful one-two punch for anyone looking to turn their baseline breathwork routine into a badass session.

The other interesting thing about a plate carrier is it makes you more aware of your circumferential breathing and will help you train to breathe through different areas of your diaphragm. With the plate carrier cinched around your torso, your best breathing is through your sides. You can expand your sides more easily, especially if in a position where more pressure is put on both your front and back. A good example is being on a bike or stationary assault bike. When leaning slightly forward you are already putting pressure on your stomach area, and the plate on your back will now further constrict breathing into your back. On a normal mountain bike ride I will breathe through my side and back; when I add the plate carrier I am using more of the sides of my diaphragm to pull air into my lungs. If you were to use this for log rolls, sit-ups, or an exercise like burpees, you will find that as the weight shifts and puts more pressure on different areas of your breathing anatomy, you will have to dynamically change what part of your diaphragm you breathe with. This is also a valuable exercise in itself; although similar work can be done without it, the plate carrier makes it almost impossible to get a good breath if you don't teach yourself to breathe through various parts of your diaphragm. It is definitely a good awareness tool which forces you to discover new levels of breathing that you may not uncover without it.

Training Mask and Plate Carrier Combined

When you put the training mask and the plate carrier together it becomes almost impossible to complete a good set of an exercise if not breathing optimally. The more difficult you make it to breathe, the more you will learn about how you can optimize your breath, including when to breathe, where to breathe, and how to breathe. As always, be cautious. Start slow when adding these tools. You should already be comfortable with breath holds and feel grounded with proper circumferential breathing and pacing before adding these tools. If you push too hard, too fast you can find yourself dizzy or passed out. Again, no weight-bearing exercise to start. I keep it simple for safety. It's badass enough on its own, trust me.

When incorporating these tools into breathwork sessions I will also occasionally switch to mouth breathing. The goal of these tools is to make breathing so difficult that it pushes you beyond your previous boundaries. These are advanced tools. You should not use them to increase the difficulty of an exercise that you cannot already perform using only nose breathing. Your first objective should be to complete any and all of your breathwork routines by breathing only through your nose. As a beginner this may be the only resistance you need. As your breathing gets past baseline, these tools can then be added to help you get to the next level. As you push up against barriers and test your limits, you will have to resort to mouth breathing as it is the only way you will be able to pull in enough air. This is that extra gear I have been talking about. Remember earlier I said that there are instances where mouth breathing will become needed. Here it comes. Thus far I have instructed you to only use nose breathing. The reason for this was to decrease CO_2 sensitivity, decrease pace, and get you habituated to using your nose as the primary ingress point for breath. Before correcting your breathing and improving your BOLT score, you may have opened your mouth to breathe doing standard pushups or burpees because your breathing needed to be fixed and your CO_2/O_2 blood chemistry corrected. If you've followed along till now and you have a BOLT score of 20 or above, then we can start talking about when it is appropriate to mouth breathe.

At this point, if you are engaged in high-intensity exercise, that goes beyond 85% of your VO2 max (the maximum amount of oxygen your body can utilize during exercise), then you can switch to mouth breathing. What is your VO2 max and how do you measure when you reach 85%? Here I rely on how I feel. I have not gone for a VO2 max test to know the exact figure. My personal rule is that once I start using these additional breathing tools, I experience an air hunger that goes beyond anything else I have experienced. Once I've used all the previous tools that we have been discussing throughout this book – circumferential breathing through the optimal parts of my diaphragm, good breathing pace and volume, nose breathing – but I still can't get enough air to keep going, I open my mouth. After experiencing this sensation, you will begin to learn when breathing through your mouth is optimal. As your VO2 max goes up you may also find that you can now complete more of these exercises without opening your mouth or delay mouth breathing to a later stage of the workout.

Remember what I said earlier. If you have been breathing through your nose, and decreased your CO_2 sensitivity, then by the time you reach this 85% point you have already released nitric oxide, dilating your blood vessels (increasing the size of the pipe that your blood travels through) and optimized your blood chemistry such that it is primed to absorb and release more bioavailable oxygen. Under these conditions, when you now take in more air through your mouth your body can use it. That is your next gear. Once you get to this point and learn through experience when to switch to mouth breathing, you will find the previously impossible, possible. That is the reason we use these tools.

Key Takeaways

- Straws can be used to train your breathing muscles, particularly your exhale muscles, by making it more difficult to force air through the straw while simultaneously decreasing breathing pace due to the fact that the straw restricts volume.

- Training masks are inspiratory flow resistant loading (IFRL) training tools that make it more difficult to take a breath, increasing the strength and adaptability of your breathing muscles.

- Masks and plate carriers can increase the intensity of any exercise, turning it into a badass breathing workout.

- These advanced tools should only be utilized if you have already reached baseline. This means that you have a BOLT score of 20 or above, have corrected your breathing patterns using only your nose and circumferential breathing, with a pace and volume that optimizes your blood chemistry for maximal oxygen absorption.

- These advanced tools, breathing patterns, and workouts are designed to take you from baseline to badass.

Core Techniques

I can incorporate the training mask or plate carrier with any exercise, but below are a few exercises that I have designed to specifically use with the training mask. I will add the plate carrier if I want to further increase the difficulty.

After completing an exercise (when using the training mask) I will attempt to recover a normal breathing pattern, leaving the mask on whatever setting I had it on when I finished the exercise. Sometimes this is not possible and I will have to click the mask to an easier setting or take it off completely. Recovering your breath using the workout setting you finished with is the goal. However, don't let this goal hinder progress. Push yourself by advancing to harder settings. This will allow you to strengthen your breathing muscles and build up to a higher setting for your recovery breaths in time.

When a mask or breathwork session is over, I will again try to recover normal breathing using the setting I ended with. Once normal breathing is restored at this setting, I will then add greater breathing resistance and leave the mask on this setting until I can maintain normal breathing. I consider my cool-down period complete if I can put the mask back into the most difficult setting while maintaining a normal breathing pace and experience only minimal air hunger.

Wind Sprints

I start each set with the training mask at the hardest setting. You should choose a setting where it is slightly difficult to breathe, even while resting. On this setting, sprint 50 yards as fast as possible. I try not to take more than one breath during this dash as it is very difficult once you are in sprint mode.

On completion of the sprint, I click the mask down by two settings. In some training masks, depending on the granularity of the adjustments, this could be going from a high to medium resistance setting. My training mask has 12 resistance settings. When I perform the sprint I am using the maximum resistance of 12. When I complete the sprint I back the resistance down to 10. At this lower setting, walk back to the start line breathing as deeply and slowly as you can. Once back at the starting line, repeat this exact sequence again.

Perform five to 10 sets of these sprints using the same pattern and training mask settings. The goal is to be able to complete each set using the same settings. If you find that your legs are really heavy, you're getting dizzy or feeling faint, then that is where training stops. Remember that this is a breathing exercise. Your objective should not be to complete a personal best sprint time or perform more sets than previously. The focus should be on your breathing. For this reason, with all the mask-aided exercises, it is important to use the correct resistance. Start with something that provides mild difficulty allowing you to complete more sets, and then add more breathing resistance for intensity.

You can also add a plate carrier to this exercise which will further increase the resistance not only on your legs but your breathing muscles, making it very difficult to recover after the sprint. While performing the sprint I tend to take only one or two breaths, and even those can be difficult when using high-resistance settings on the mask. To spare my breathing muscles I will even resort to a breath hold at the start, take a short breath in the middle, followed by another breath hold till I reach the finish line. It is not a standard hold where I am gauging air hunger; I am just minimizing the use of my breathing muscles during the run itself. The recovery is where all the good circumferential breathing happens and where you get to really strengthen those primary breathing muscles.

Assault/Stationary Bike

Choose a steady pace that you can keep for five minutes at moderate difficulty. Do not select a pace that you would normally struggle with as this will make it very difficult to complete the entire exercise. Most stationary bikes or assault bikes have a monitor that gauges speed or cadence. The goal is to stick to the same cadence throughout this exercise. Start with the mask at a difficult setting (at which it is fairly difficult to breathe even at rest). Cycle at a moderate pace for 75 seconds. At this point (without stopping), click down two settings on the mask (exactly as you did in the sprint exercise above) or from high resistance to a medium resistance. Keeping the same pace, continue on this setting for 45 seconds. You should now be at the two-minute mark. Click the mask back to the difficult setting for 15 seconds and then decrease the resistance two clicks (or to medium depending on your mask settings) for 45 seconds. Perform this same pattern with the same settings for five minutes, keeping a constant pace.

There are multiple ways to increase resistance for this exercise. You can add a plate carrier, which will increase the difficulty of breathing due to the pressure it will put on your midsection. You can increase the amount of time you keep the mask at maximum. For instance, I will keep the whole exercise to five minutes for a week but each day I will increase the time the mask is at the maximum setting by five seconds. So, when I reach the two-minute mark I will do 20 seconds at the maximum mask setting on day two, 25 on day three, 30 on day four, 35 on day five. This obviously reduces the recovery time when the mask is at a moderate setting. On day five you only have 25 seconds to recover, which means you are spending more time at the maximum setting than at the recovery setting. This becomes a very difficult exercise to complete. You can then increase the cadence speed and/or increase the length of time you perform the exercise. I never go beyond 10 minutes as this is meant to be a breathing exercise that is focused on intensity. But there are multiple ways to increase the resistance and difficulty.

This is one of my favorite exercises because you are on a stationary bike, the cadence is easy to gauge, and it is easy to click the mask while exercising. This means that you can focus completely on how you breathe. The more resistance you add, the more you will learn about your breath because it will become impossible to complete the exercise without maximizing your breathing performance. When the mask is at maximum you will feel how your diaphragm moves; you will feel where there is tension and move the breath to other parts of the diaphragm in order to optimize breathing. This is definitely one to try.

Burpees

This is another one of my favorites because it is difficult to breath during normal execution as you go from standing to plank, pushup, then back to standing, adding a little jump at the end for good measure. Therefore, you have to push your breath into different areas of your diaphragm during the execution. If you use a plate carrier, this adds additional strain and restrictions to those areas that are the best places to breathe, forcing you to strengthen those muscles.

I start out with the most difficult mask setting and continue to do burpees until I feel I really can't breathe anymore. Again, as with all these exercises I am focusing on the breath not on counting repetitions. If you want to gauge progress I suggest getting someone else to count or use a timer instead of rep count. As soon as I get caught up in counting I lose focus on how I am breathing. Once I get to a point where I can't breathe, I let up on the mask two clicks and then keep going. I keep doing burpees until I have gone through all the settings on the mask, lessening the air resistance by two clicks each time I feel like I can't go on. Once I'm at the minimum resistance I will continue until I just can't perform any more burpees.

This exercise is difficult because you never really catch your breath, and if you are in good shape it can go on for a while, so you start to train your body and mind to deal with air hunger for longer durations. Decreasing the resistance after reaching a point where you feel you can't get enough air may feel great initially, but it is short lived. You will be able to breathe easier, but you quickly realize you will never really catch your breath. You will experience moderate to severe air hunger throughout the entire exercise until you are almost at the end, and by that time your body is exhausted. If that is how it feels when you perform this, and you are cursing the day you read this, congratulations, you performed it perfectly.

Calisthenics

Pullups, chin-ups, pushups, air squats. These are simple exercises where I use a combination of the above training-mask and plate-carrier patterns to increase the difficulty. As one example, I will either use the max setting on the training mask to do as many pullups as I can then decrease the resistance on the mask by two clicks for the recovery period but also for the next set. I will then continue to drop the breathing resistance on the mask by two clicks for each subsequent set until I reach my target number of sets for that exercise or will keep performing sets until the mask is at its easiest setting.

Another option is to adopt the same principle that I used for burpees above to perform any exercise of your choice. Do one continuous set on the max setting, then decrease the breathing resistance

on the mask whenever you experienced extreme air hunger. Continue
to follow this pattern until failure.

Advanced Techniques

The plate carrier and mask have innumerable variations that you
can play with in order to constantly change how you are breathing
and increase breathing resistance, thereby improving your breathing
performance. If you crave more advanced techniques, fool around
with rep-counts, timing, and the breathing resistance on the mask to
make exercises more difficult to complete. Another option to increase
difficulty is to include breath holds for a number of reps followed by
normal breathing with the mask at a difficult setting. If you up the
intensity of your workout and decrease rest periods, you will reach
your VO2 max and be forced to breathe through your mouth. Once
you've reached this level of intensity, you are well on your way to
badass.

As I am constantly devising new exercises, utilizing the latest tools
and technology, I suggest you visit to stay up to date on my newest
breathwork routines.

CHAPTER 9 - BASELINE TO BADASS - A TYPICAL DAY AND WEEK IN THE BREATHING LIFE OF A BADASS

In this chapter I will explain how I incorporate breathwork into my daily and weekly routine. My goal was to seamlessly integrate breathwork into my life so that it would become automatic and would not feel like I had to set aside specific times to do it. With the exception of a morning breathing session and one focused breathwork session a week (30-40 minutes) all other breathwork was incorporated during periods of sitting in the car waiting for my children (dance lessons), while reading, relaxing, or during or after my workouts. I am not going to go through my workout routine in detail, that is for a future book, but I will focus on how I include breathwork into those routines. Finally, I will show you how I then incorporate the use of training masks and plate carriers to increase intensity or lower volume in my workouts while demonstrating how I use them to perform specific exercises.

These are all suggestions. I hope they provide an example and not a program. As I stated at the beginning of this book, my goal is to provide the basic knowledge and create a framework that gives you, the reader, the flexibility to find your own path and develop a program and routine that works for you. Depending on your current level, you can start with just one or two suggestions and work your way up from there. Also, the exercises you use will depend on your goals and what you want to achieve. That is why I stress the framework concept. The core ideas in this book and in this routine can work to improve breathing muscle strength, pattern and pace control, decrease sensitivity to CO_2 and lactic acid, increase nitric oxide production, and better your overall cardio and muscular performance. Armed with that you can weaponize this knowledge to fit your lifestyle and goals. Let's get to it.

DAILY

Morning

Wim Hof method – I will use different variations each day as I described in the Advanced Techniques section of Chapter 1.

After completing the Wim Hof method I will perform one breath-hold exercise such as those I reviewed in Chapter 7. This is to ensure that I do not build a sensitivity to CO_2, as the Wim Hof method will delay the buildup of CO_2 which can result in CO_2 sensitivity if not balanced with another exercise.

While reading in the morning I will breathe very slowly and deeply while occasionally switching to small flickers of breath that just barely fill my nose. At times I will also perform breath holds on empty lungs and see how many paragraphs I can read before I have to take a slow breath in. I will usually do this for 10-15 minutes. This is a great way to work on slowing your breathing pace and lowering volume while also getting in some breath holds to decrease CO_2 sensitivity.

Throughout the Day and Evening

Be aware of your breathing and how it affects your mood and performance. Modify your breathing to meet the demands of the situation. This could be hyperventilation to oxygenate your body and brain for a high-performance task or slowing your pace or performing box breathing to de-stress.

If you are still at a stage where you are working to correct bad breathing habits then I suggest checking in with your breath regularly to ensure you are nose breathing, diaphragm breathing, and controlling the pace. Start out with more frequent check-ins, maybe every 15 minutes, and reduce these as proper breathing become more automatic.

When I am relaxing, either reading or waiting in the car to pick up my children from some activity, I will perform breath holds, slow breathing, limited breathing, or box breathing.

In addition, when preparing for a race or competition I will typically begin wearing a mask for a certain amount of time a day during normal daily activities. As mentioned previously, I may wear it while doing yardwork or mowing the lawn but at other times I may use it while writing or even watching television. (My wife doesn't like the noise when we watch television together, at which point I remind her that I no longer snore. This diminishes some of the complaints, but not all.)

Again, use the mask sensibly. Just like any tool it can be overused. To get your muscles stronger you need to engage in resistance training;

but if you do it too often you never recover, which results in over-training. Same principle applies to breathwork. Your cardiorespiratory system needs time to recover as well. Progress is better made slowly and consistently.

Exercise Routines and Breathwork

Most of the year I exercise five or six days a week, with two or three days of strength training, one or two days of cardio-specific work, and then one or two days of sport-related activities such as mountain biking and/or jiujitsu training. The amount of each will depend on the specifics of the current training cycle. There are times when I will actually have multiple sessions in a single day. The point being that no matter how many times I work out or which cycle I am in, before per-forming any of these activities I utilize the below breathwork warmup and also incorporate some of the breathwork exercises into many of these routines.

Exercise Warmup

Perform 40 Wim Hof-style hyperventilation breaths but with no breath holds. This will get you oxygenated and awake. Perform these breaths through your nose and you will also get the benefits of nitric oxide release, such as vasodilation.

Alternatively, or in conjunction with hyperventilation, use nasal humming to increase nitric oxide release.

During Exercise

Add a breath hold at the end of the workout or perform the last set of each exercise with a few repetitions of breath holds (non-load bearing exercises). This can also be flipped using the breath holds as part of the warm-up set for a particular exercise, allowing you to focus on the breath. This is particularly useful if you are performing high-intensity sets which you do not want to disrupt with a breath hold. Breath holds during your workout will decrease your CO_2 and lactic-acid sensitivity.

Exercise Cool Down

During the cool-down period I will usually perform another breathing exercise, alternating which exercise I use throughout the week. This will usually consist of an exercise like the pulse-timing Systema technique where I coordinate my pulse with slower breathing cycles to slow my heartrate, as described in Chapter 6. Another option is to perform box breathing with my legs up, as described in Chapter 2. You can substitute any exercise you want, but it should be focused on getting you cooled down and relaxed so that you can start to recover from your workout.

WEEKLY

10-20 Minutes at the End of a Workout

At the end of one workout a week I will devote 10-20 minutes to breathing exercises. This can be any of the breath holds or restricted-breathing exercises found in this book. As an example, you could perform the assault-bike exercise with a training mask and then add the training mask with burpees, both described in Chapter 8, and/or a few sets of pushups, pullups or squats using the one-for-one ratio breathing, as described in Chapter 7. As I continually stress, these exercises should be focused on breathing (or not breathing), not on the activity itself. We want to task our breathing anatomy and chemistry not our musculature.

One Breathwork-Focused Session

Once a week I devote 30-40 minutes to a breathwork-only session. This is performed when rested, not after having completed another standard workout. I want to have all my physical and mental resources ready to concentrate purely on improving my breathing. This is where I will combine many of the techniques covered in this book in a single session. Breath holds, running with mask and vest, Systema exercises, diaphragm strengthening, etc. The point here is to devote time to the breathing apparatus without already being tired after a workout. This allows you to devote the full resources of mind and body on improving your breathing performance. I try to use a mix of holds, movement, breathing disruptions with odd timing, Systema exercises like bundled breathing, burst breathing, slow repetitions, etc., combined with rolls, martial arts moves, running, tumbling, etc. adding masks, vests, straws as needed to increase difficulty.

Rinse. Wash. Repeat.

Focused Breathing Opportunities

One unique opportunity to focus on breathwork is if you are suffering from an injury or recovering after a competition and can't perform at 100% in your chosen sport or activity. As an example, I had a mountain bike accident that damaged my kneecap and kept me from doing heavy squats or participating in jiujitsu. This left a lot of time to devote to breathwork. I've found these concentrated periods of time can really push you to the next level. Instead of doing one session of 30-40 minutes of breathwork, I was doing three or four.

After I cracked my ribs in a snowboarding accident, I took the opportunity to focus on limiting volume and pacing. I used the pain of expanding my ribs to provide the motivation to limit my breathing cadence and depth, which went a long way towards increasing my CO2 tolerance.

Short of an injury, I suggest having a focused week or two devoted to breathwork at least twice a year but preferably once a quarter. This will elevate you to the next level, which you will then maintain through your daily and weekly breathwork routines the rest of the year. These focused weeks will usually be coordinated with my workout cycle during times when I am decreasing volume or in a phase of active recovery. During these weeks I will dedicate three or four 30- to 40-minute sessions to bringing my breathing to the next level using all the tools and techniques discussed in this book.

Log It

Logging your workouts and your breathwork is a great way to monitor progress and keep track of the particular exercises, repetitions, and tools (mask settings, plate carrier weights, etc.) you are using. It ensures that you are keeping up with your breathwork and varying it enough to hit all the areas of breathing we have covered in this book. Make sure to include your BOLT scores to show your progress. If you don't log, you won't have an accurate reference. Progress is our goal, so log it.

If you would like to see the details of my particular breathwork schedule and timing, visit and download my free breathwork calendar which details the breathwork I completed over the course of a month. This will give you an idea of how to frame your own calendar based on your needs and goals.

AFTERWORD

This is just the beginning of your journey, one that I hope will make you feel grateful for every breath and give you the desire to make every breath count. In addition, I hope that once you reach critical mass in your breathwork and see your progress you will commit time and resources to not only improving your breath but begin to broaden your scope to improving other areas of your life, like diet, exercise, relationships, and spirituality. In my experience, once you see that your investment pays off you will want to invest more in becoming more.

I hope this book has achieved its aim in providing you with the core knowledge and exercises that will take you from bad to badass. The purpose of this book was not to dissect breathing anatomy and biology or give an exhaustive list of all the exercises available. For those interested in learning more, I have provided a list of resources at that will take you deeper into any area of breathing you are passionate about. These resources contain information that I recommend to anyone who wants to learn more about breathing physiology, breathing science, or breathwork. With that said, I do believe that the information in this book alone can take you from bad to baseline to badass.

This journey towards becoming a better version of myself began with breath because that was my weakest link. It was improper breathing that became a limiting factor in reaching the goals I had set for myself. Seven years later, I am still doing breathwork on a daily basis. I have competed in more than 30 obstacle-course races, continue to mountain bike, and train every day. I also started training in Brazilian jujitsu, which has been a dream of mine for 20 years. My fear of not being able to breathe and my experience with wrestling in high school made me believe that Brazilian jiujitsu was something I would just have to include in the list of activities I just wasn't built for. But after fixing my breathing, and then later my diet and exercise, I am no longer bound by physical limitations, only mental ones. Having been given an amazing gift by coming across the knowledge shared in these pages, I no longer wanted to regret not trying new things. With that in mind I decided to sign up for classes at a local school, and I can say that I am so grateful that I didn't let my fear stop me.

To paraphrase one of my favorite motivational speakers Jocko Willink, Getting better is not changing one thing, it is a campaign. I agree. However, I suggest that you at least start with one thing. Once you begin to see the change, allow it to grow into a campaign. As I said in the beginning, this is not a system or a program; this will not fix every aspect of your life. But, in my opinion it's a great place to start your journey to becoming badass.

WHERE TO LEARN MORE ABOUT BREATHING

T o continue to learn more and stay up to date with the newest books, information, exercises and breathing tools please visit www.badtobadass.com. In addition visit www.badtobadass.com /ajourneyinbreath, to see additional material including a gallery of pictures that demonstrate the exercises in this book, recommended reading list for badass breathers that want to learn more, as well as information about the various masks and gear that I use in my breathwork.

Get started with your breathwork **TODAY** and visit:

https://www.badtobadass.com/free30daybadassbreathingroutine to download your **FREE** copy of my **30-Day Badass Breathing Routine**.

ABOUT THE BADASS JOURNEY

This series is not meant to be an exhaustive explanation of the various topics covered. Each book has been designed to provide the tools, knowledge, and inspiration to start your own journey. In each book of this series I boil down what has worked for me, including the core information, skills, and techniques I applied to get me from bad to badass. As with all journeys of discovery, there is always more to learn and experience. This book and the others that will follow provide the desire, inspiration, and tools that will get you far down the road, providing immediate benefits. I've taken my many years of trial and error in various techniques and exercises and condensed what I have learned into a concise plan of action so you can share the same benefits I gained.

That is my sole aim. To enthuse and inspire people to better themselves as simply and easily as possible. I urge you to try and apply some of these techniques to your life and see how they work. If you persist for long enough to push past critical mass, I am sure you will become committed to learn and do more.

I've shared within these books my journey. My journey can't be yours; only you can walk the path, and it will differ from mine. This is a framework not a program. I came to realize all journeys are personal and what works for one person may not for another; but the core of what is needed to get there is contained in these books. So, let's take a few steps together and see where we get. I'd hazard to guess you'll end up further down your chosen path than you were before you picked up this book. Good luck. I look forward to seeing you on the path.

BECOME A BAD-TO-BADASS NEWSLETTER SUBSCRIBER

L ike everything else on this journey, my breathing is an evolution. I am constantly learning and applying new techniques. At some point maybe I will have enough to create an additional breathing book, but if you would like to stay abreast of my evolution in breathing or in any of my other areas of focus in the meantime, you can join the bad to badass newsletter where I share any updates on techniques in various areas including breathing as well as any news about upcoming events or books at www.badtobadass.com/subscription

HOW TO SUPPORT THE BAD-TO-BADASS MOVEMENT

- Become badass yourself and share with others how you did it.

- Send me an email to info@badtobadass.com and let me know how this book helped or what you thought could have been better.

- Rate and leave a review with Amazon. This helps spread the word and is crucial to getting the books noticed so that others can find them.

- Follow us on social media at www.facebook.com/badtobadass and subscribe to our newsletter www.badtobadass.com/subscription

- It's great to become badass but even better to become part of an entire community of badass people that understand the journey and how to continue it. Join us on social media (www.facebook.com/badtobadass) to help others start down a path of becoming better versions of themselves. Let's encourage each other to be better, as individuals, as a community, as friends. We are all in this together, and if we don't start helping each other in a positive direction we will be lost; and that just wouldn't be badass.

Made in the USA
Monee, IL
30 January 2025

11274163R00079